Play GOLF *forever*

More Praise for Dr. Michael Jaffe and *Play Golf Forever:*

"Being familiar with lower back pain, I am most impressed with the comprehensive approach the author takes. This practical and well-focused text is packed with critical information for making golf a healthy and enjoyable life-time activity."
—*Jeffery M. Johnston, Director of Golf, University of California at Irvine*

"This informative book is a must for physicians and golfers alike. The book stresses the importance of biomechanics for a good golf swing to prevent injury, and the treatment of injury thereafter."
—*Brian Davis, MD, Director Sports and Spine Center, Department of Physical Medicine and Rehabilitation, University of California at Davis Medical Center*

"I was not able to play golf due to a 10-year history of low back pain. Our Medical Director suggested that I see Dr. Jaffe. He placed me on this Golf Fitness program, and I have been playing golf two times a week ever since."
—*Julie Phillipson, MD, Pathologist*

"I have used Dr. Jaffe's program to treat many patients. The proof is in my practice. This program will strengthen the muscles that you need to support your low back and control your golf swing."
—*Sharon Kyle, RPT, Physical Therapist*

PLAY GOLF FOREVER

Treating Low Back Pain and Improving Your Golf Swing through Fitness

Michael Jaffe, DO
with Brian Tarcy
and Ron Brizzie, DO

LITERARY™
ARCHITECTS

Play Golf Forever: Treating Low Back Pain and Improving Your Golf Swing through Fitness

Black-and-white trade edition.

Published by:
Literary Architects
1075 Broad Ripple Ave, Suite 353
Indianapolis, IN 46220
www.literaryarchitects.com

Copyright © 2006 by Michael Jaffe, DO.

International Standard Book Number: 1-933669-00-4

Library of Congress Catalog Card Number: Available upon request.

Printed in the United States of America.

Note: This publication contains the opinions and ideas of its author. It is intended to provide helpful and informative material on the subject matter covered. It is sold with the understanding that the author and publisher are not engaged in rendering professional services in the book. If the reader required personal assistance or advice, a competent professional should be consulted.

For information on publicity, marketing, or selling this book, contact Bryan Gambrel, Marketing Director, Literary Architects, 812-336-5333. For information on becoming a Literary Architects author, contact Renee Wilmeth, Acquisitions Director, 317-925-7045. For information on working for Literary Architects, contact Timothy Ryan, Publishing Director, 317-596-0049.

www.literaryarchitects.com

www.playgolfforever.com

Cover design: Kelly Hines Keller, GrafikNature
Front & back cover background image: copyright Wonderfile Corporation
Interior design and composition: Amy Hassos
Copyediting: Tiffany Taylor
Proofreading: Julie Campbell
Index: Angie Bess

This book is dedicated with love to my wife, Linda, and my daughters, Brin and Jenna. Your devotion and understanding allowed me to start writing this book at the beginning of the most arduous time of our lives—parenthood.

Acknowledgements

Brian Tarcy—Thank you for all of your collaboration on this project. I may have written a book, but you are truly a writer.

Ron Brizzie, DO—You were the inspiration for this whole project. It is wonderful to see the student surpass the teacher. Your future is so bright, you had better wear shades.

Bruce Bekkar, MD—Mentor, friend, stand-up comic.

Franz and Yoana Snideman—*Revolution Fitness Center*. You are two of the best physical exercise trainers on the planet.

Demitrus Willis—*Drive Fitness Design*. Thank you for introducing me to the world of functional training. You are truly a pioneer in the field.

Frank Nienstedt—You're the best golf partner anyone could ask for.

Special thank-you to: Bernard Jaffe for your encouragement; Matt Kuehnert, PT; Garth and Kim Getchell; Siri Johansson; Mike Snell; and Elizabeth Baldwin.

Table of Contents

Introduction

Golfing Forever with Functional Training

When Fred Couples' notoriously bad back flared up, forcing him to withdraw from the Chrysler Championship in October 2003, he stood at number 32 on the PGA money list. He was looking to make a lot of money.

The Chrysler championship was his last tournament and last chance to qualify for the top 30 money leaders and the Tour Championship. The price Couples paid for his bad back measured in tens of thousands of dollars or more, depending on how he might have played. Tens of thousands of dollars!

Missing the tournament was certainly a high price for a bad back, but thousands of amateur golfers pay an even higher price for their bad backs: They quit golfing completely. For those who live to golf, this is indeed the highest price.

Golfers of all sorts dream of a magic pill to make their backs feel better; but that pill, unfortunately, doesn't exist. Still, patients always ask me for it. There must be a way to stop the pain, they say. In fact, there is a way, a better way—the power of the body to heal itself.

Most people who quit golf because of low back pain could keep golfing if they understood the power they possess to strengthen their own backs. *Functional training*, in which the entire body is retrained to work as a unit, is the program that can get you back on the golf course. And, as a great side benefit, it actually improves your golf swing. Functional training is a magic pill—only you don't *take* it, you do it.

The Conundrum: Oh, My Aching Back

At some point in life, low back pain is part of the human experience for almost everyone. For known and unknown reasons, low back pain is one of the unfortunate ties that bind us together in this journey on Earth.

Of course, knowing that others share your pain offers little relief to you. And even within the commonality of the experience are unique circumstances of each individual's back. Everyone is different, and the hardest part for doctors and patients to understand is that a clear correlation doesn't always exist between what the back shows in x-rays or Magnetic Resonance Image (MRI) scans and how the patient feels.

Low back pain (LBP) is a conundrum.

Sometimes, there is no logical explanation. Some people have x-rays or MRI scans that show damage to the structure of the back, but the patients have no symptoms. Other patients have severe symptoms with no obvious causes that show up in scans. For doctors, this situation is frustrating and somewhat bizarre.

This is not to say that a closer look—by MRI or x-ray—isn't helpful. It can often be very useful. But the truth is that what shows up on a picture doesn't necessarily reflect how the patient feels.

The truth is that the back is a complicated mechanism, and when problems occur, there are no easy answers.

The back basically provides strength, movement, and stability; but the cause of any specific pain in the back can be difficult to find, because the system itself—bones, nerves, ligaments, and muscles—is so intricate. Any movement requires a combination of actions throughout the system. A complex movement, such as a perfect golf swing, requires that the back work like a finely tuned machine.

In most humans, the design of the back begins without flaws. Parts wear with time, but often, simple maintenance is the best solution to low back pain.

Some Numbers: You Are Not Alone

The fact that you have LBP is not, in itself, a reason to worry. As the following numbers show, it happens to almost everyone:

- About 80 percent of the population will experience LBP at some point in their lives.

- Up to 85 percent of those with LBP cannot be given a definitive diagnosis because of weak associations between symptoms and test results such as x-rays and MRI.

- LBP is the most common reason for someone under 45 to go on disability.

It is the weak associations between symptoms and test results that make treating LBP especially difficult. That is why functional training is the only true magic bullet. That, and time.

More Numbers: Without Treatment, Most LBP Gets Better

It's true. Low back pain comes and goes; it usually doesn't last. Consider these statistics:

- 90 percent of acute LBP resolves in four to six weeks.

- An additional 5 percent resolves by 12 weeks.

- Only 5 percent of low back pain becomes chronic.

- Fifty percent of those with acute LBP have a recurrence within one year.

If you have a flare-up, you can be reasonably sure that it will go away by itself. The body is a wonderful natural healing machine.

It doesn't always heal itself, of course. But your confidence in your body's ability to heal itself should be as high, or higher, than in any doctor's ability to heal you. Your body is the real miracle worker.

A clear path doesn't always exist from pain to recovery.

In fact, this road usually isn't a clear path at all, but rather a sort of rollercoaster in which the body takes two steps forward for every step back. You may have a painful time for four to six weeks, but the pain should begin to lessen within 10 days—although flare-ups will occur. I often chart the recovery process like this:

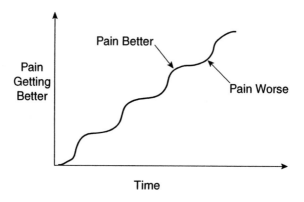

This graph doesn't mean that everyone follows this path. Rather, the chart shows what is typical. LBP is a conundrum, and everyone's experience is completely unique. But one truth is universal: *functional training can help.*

Still More Numbers: Returning to Work

Activity is good:

- Only 50 percent of people return to work when they are off for six months.

- Only 25 percent return to work when they are off for one year.

- Zero percent (zero!) return to work after being off for more than two years.

I have had patients ask me for disability from work due to their LBP, which is fine for a short period of time. But, as the above numbers show, patients with long-term disability from work due to LBP tend to do worse about going back to work.

It may seem like a good thing to go on long-term disability. It may seem like a good thing to get plenty of rest. In some cases, for a short while, rest is good. But if you lose your reason to get out of bed, and you are not a productive member of society, you are going to do *much worse* in the long run.

Rest ≠ Treatment

Falling into disability is a sad process in which the patient loses a reason for life, becomes depressed, and focuses increasingly on the pain. To make matters worse, the patient can become dependent on others. The cycle causes the patient to do even less and become more depressed.

There is a way out.

The good news is that there is a flip side to these numbers. If you stay active, you are liable to remain active. You are in charge.

You can do it.

Introducing Functional Training

Moving and manipulating your body is an instinctive/learned skill. After you are born, you learn to creep, and then you learn to crawl. You learn to walk. You learn to run. That is maturation, and with each progressive step taken in your early days, you train your body as well as respond instinctively.

A healthy body naturally learns to do many things. But over time, a healthy body can run into problems, and parts can wear out.

The biggest problem occurs when a healthy body becomes a not-so-healthy body. This can happen when you neglect to do simple maintenance to keep your body tuned up for the rigors of life—and golf!

For years, you probably never thought you needed to do any maintenance. Sure, the very best athletes need to tune their bodies, but you are a weekend warrior. You have better things to do, right?

Actually, *there is nothing better that you can do* for your body than to embark on a program of functional training. It is the best exercise program on the planet.

What is functional training?

Functional training is a conditioning program that trains your entire body to be functional. Pretty simple, huh?

Yes, it is. Because the body is complex, you need to exercise your body as a unit. When you understand how your body and the back work, you can then target muscle groups that over time can be strengthened to protect the back.

Functional training is not a pill. It's you, moving.

It's you, exercising.

It's you.

It's up to you.

Functional training is the greatest exercise program in the world, and it works on low back pain for golfers of any age. If certain movements with your job or hobbies are repetitive, these exercises will benefit you as well. Functional training works because it makes sense.

Functional training is different because it targets things that aren't typically targeted. It targets things besides strength. Golfers need more. Humans need more. Functional training also targets *balance* and *manipulative skills*.

After all, a golf swing is a quick, almost violent action performed by the back muscles. There is a lot involved, including a lot of stress.

Functional training fine-tunes all the things involved in a golf swing:

- Stability
- Locomotor movement (moving the body)
- Manipulative movement (using an object, such as a 5-iron)

The program involves objects such as bars, stability balls, medicine balls, and weights.

It targets the *core muscles* around the abdoi
The core muscles include the abdominal muscles (e
abdominal muscle transversus abdominus), the mu
such as the buttock muscles, and the back muscles
strengthened, they act as shock absorbers for your s

Although this is a program for golfers, by also ta geting balance, the program brings added advantages to all areas of life.

For instance, functional training challenges your *righting instinct,* which is your natural instinct to catch yourself if you are about to fall. When that instinct is challenged, it becomes stronger. This helps in going up the stairs as well as standing on the side of a hill with a golf club in your hands.

Functional training, when you embark upon it seriously, is a life-changing program. You will literally feel younger, stronger, better. It's like the old TV program, "The Six Million Dollar Man." Only this is no scientist talking. It's you. You have the ability. You can do it.

This is how.

Par for the Course: A Summary

- Low back pain is a conundrum because it is often hard to match symptoms with test results.
- Most people have LBP at some time in their life.
- Most LBP gets better over time without treatment.
- Rest does not equal treatment. Activity is good.
- Functional training, in which the entire body is trained to work as a unit, is the best thing you can do for LBP.

Part

The Back

Understanding Low Back Pain (LBP)

When I first met Julia in my office, her obvious athleticism contrasted with her chronic low back pain (LBP).

It seemed wrong. She was in great shape. Everyone gets occasional LBP, but Julia's developed into a chronic condition that had lasted for years by the time she came to see me. A "back specialist" diagnosed her with bulging and degenerative disks and told her to limit her activities.

Initially, Julia's back pain appeared only when she engaged in physical activity. But when she limited her activities, her problems worsened. She became sedentary, gained 15 pounds, and suffered continuous pain. Her job as a pathologist required that she sit at a microscope for nine hours each day, making the situation worse. Plus, the rest she was prescribed compounded her problem.

When Julia learned the core-strengthening program taught in this book and put it to use, her pain finally began to subside. It took time—six weeks of squat exercises—but by the time I saw her again, she had already lost five pounds and felt much better.

Julia's case proved again to me what I already knew—that there are many types of back pain, and even those who are in great shape can get LBP. Being in shape and having your core muscles in shape are sometimes different things.

Seeing Health

We express ourselves with our bones and our muscles. We don't express ourselves through our internal organs. You don't often hear someone say, "You have a nice spleen."

We express ourselves through motion.

> Eighty-five percent of the neurological and sensory input that goes from your body to your brain comes from your musculoskeletal system of bones, joints, tendons, ligaments, and muscles. Only 15 percent come from your internal organs.

This expression of motion comes across to others in little ways and big ways all the time in your life. When you challenge yourself, such as on a golf course, the expression is exaggerated.

The way you move says a lot about you.

Think about it. When a healthy person walks into a room, you can tell the difference immediately between that person and one who is out of shape. Being able to execute movements with optimum speed, precision, style, and grace is an attractive trait. The person who walks into a room with their head held up has style. You can see it, as opposed to the person who is schlubby and withdrawn. You notice the difference, and it sends you a huge message.

You can pick out an athlete because of the way they move and their pure confidence of movement.

And you can train yourself to be an athlete. You can train your core muscles to give you strength and grace in your whole body. Although the body can be trained to do many different things, including swing a golf club, almost all athleticism has a centerpiece: the spine and its movements.

Your back is one of the most amazing creations in the natural world, and all athleticism flows off of it. So, like Julia, at the beginning of this chapter, if you take care of training for your particular sport but ignore the core muscle group that allows you to do anything, you can, over time, run into trouble.

If you are going to train for golf, the core muscle group supporting your lower back is where it all starts. This beautiful system of bones, muscles, ligaments, and joints is susceptible to problems that can be avoided by means of a strengthening program.

Taking care of your back and the muscles supporting it will help protect you from having pain, and it will improve your back if you do have pain.

Of course, as common as LBP is, not all LBP is the same. The back is a complex structure with many moving parts. So before treating your pain, you must first understand how the back works when you aren't suffering from pain.

The Neuromuscular System

The human body inspires awe.

And the back as a unit, performing its many functions, is a wonder within the miracle body. The spine and its supporting muscles and tendons serve as a highway and interchange for nerves that bring the feel of life to all parts of your body.

When your back does things, you almost never consciously think about it. But if you think about it now, that's pretty amazing.

You have a huge instrument running through the center of your torso, and it performs seemingly all on its own. It is able to do things reflexively, instantaneously, without you ever having to tell it how. It just knows.

Amazing.

The Big Picture

The brain does not recognize individual muscles.

It recognizes patterns of movements—movements that are, in a sense, programmed by you over time. A pattern of movement involves individual muscles working in harmony to produce movement.

But the muscles don't work alone to produce movement from your back. The back is a complex, amazing instrument capable of producing big movements with a combination of power and flexibility. But what is really happening is rather intricate.

It starts with your spinal cord, of course, because that delivers life. But the back is more than just the cord of nerves running up to your brain. There's a lot more to it than a simple straight line. The back carries the signals that shoot to nerves and on to muscles that make movement possible. The complex machinery includes the following parts:

- The cord itself is encased in bones (vertebrae).
- The vertebrae rest on discs, which cushion the bones.
- Inside the discs is a jelly-like material.
- The back part of your vertebrae have smaller bones, connected by tiny *facet joints*. These joints are found throughout your entire spine.
- Nerves come out between the bones, and muscles wrap the bones while also supporting the entire spine.

- Ligaments connect bones to bones.
- Tendons connect muscles to bones.

Although there is only one spinal cord, the working of the back is complex machinery with many moving and stationary parts.

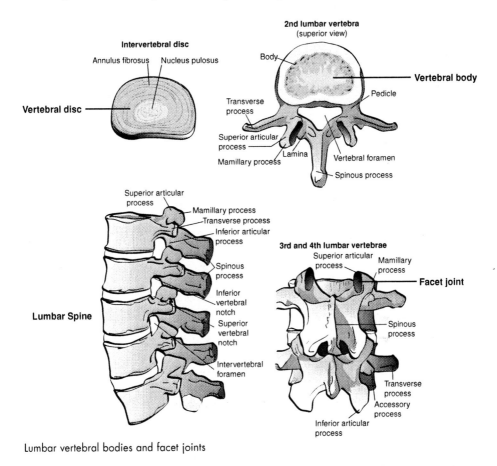

Lumbar vertebral bodies and facet joints

"Lumbar" and Other Definitions

Before we continue, let's define a few common terms. Following are the parts of your body that comprise your lumbar region and that will be discussed in this book:

Lumbar spine—The five vertebrae that form your lower back. The lumbar region is the part of the spine that is below your ribs and above your pelvis.

Facet—The joints of the spine. The joints have joint lining and joint fluid that can become inflamed just like a larger joint such as a knee joint.

Disc annulus—The outer two-thirds of the spine disc, made up of tough, connective tissue. Tears in this tissue can be painful.

Nucleus pulposis—The inner one-third of a disc, made up of a gelatinous material. This is the material that leaks out of herniated discs and is irritating to spinal nerves. A leak leads to an inflammatory response.

Transversus abdominus—A sheet of muscle that runs across your lower abdomen. This is the cornerstone muscle for core strengthening.

Rectus abdominus—Muscles that form the center of your abdomen. These are your six-pack muscles.

External abdominal oblique—Abdominal muscles that make up the side walls of your abdomen. These fibers run diagonally down from your side to your belly button.

Internal abdominal oblique—Abdominal muscles that make up the inner layer of your abdominal wall. These muscle fibers run in the opposite direction of the external abdominal oblique.

What You Can't Control

You cannot control time.

Unfortunately, the human body is not designed to last forever, and the spine is especially susceptible to wear because you use it all the time to support yourself. Bone rubs on discs. Cells break down in all of your muscles, bones, and joints.

All humans, whether they have pain symptoms or not, experience some natural deterioration of the bone and disc structure. There really is such a thing as natural wear and tear.

What You Can Control

The human body is awe-inspiring, but you have to take care of it or it can fail you.

One of the first things you can control is your weight. Your weight has a major effect on LBP because carrying around extra weight forces muscles to work harder to support you, causing extra strain.

If you have extra weight, chances are that your muscles are not as toned to carry the weight as they would be if you didn't have the weight in the first place.

Maintaining a healthy weight is only part of what you can do.

Just as important is embarking on a fitness program—a functional training program that focuses on your whole body working as a unit. A functional training program targets core muscles that support the spine, and it challenges flexibility and balance to increase your ability in both areas.

There is a lot you can control when it comes to lower back health. But even with the best program, you can end up in pain.

Defining Pain

Lower back pain is divided into three different types:

* *Acute*—Acute pain lasts less than three weeks. It's caused when you bend or twist, and you actually sprain your back. Ouch! But it goes away. It hurts, it bothers you, and in three weeks or so, you are done with it. This is the most common type of LBP.

- *Subacute*—Subacute pain lasts longer than three weeks. It lasts three months, for whatever reason. Such an injury takes a while to go away, and it doesn't heal quickly, but it does get better.

- *Chronic*—Chronic pain lasts longer than three months. People can have chronic back pain on a daily basis; or they can have recurrent pain, which means it goes and comes back very quickly. Patients with chronic pain are those who end up with a lot of disability.

Acute pain can develop into chronic, long-lasting pain, but unless you suffer an obvious permanent injury, acute pain can be expected to get better.

A little rest can help, but a lot of rest can hurt. With all three types of pain, activity is necessary to begin the healing and strengthening process.

The Vague Term, "Sciatica"

A common term is thrown around a lot with regard to LBP: sciatica.

The interesting thing about sciatica is that, well, it doesn't actually exist. I mean the term is sort of a wastebasket word for a number of problems that stem from an irritation to the largest nerve in your body, your sciatic nerve. This nerve is made up of two nerves that start in your back, go down your buttock and the back of your thigh, and go down the calf and into the foot. When you sit and you have back pain, you feel your sciatic nerve. *Sciatica* is a general term that doesn't describe any medical diagnosis.

The Misnomer, "Slipped Disc"

There is no such thing as a slipped disc. The discs are securely anchored to the bones of the spine and do not slip out of place. The term is incorrectly used to describe two different problems: a lumbar vertebral disc that has become wider (bulged backwards or to one side), or internal disc material that has herniated outside of the disc's tough outer layers.

Sciatic nerve

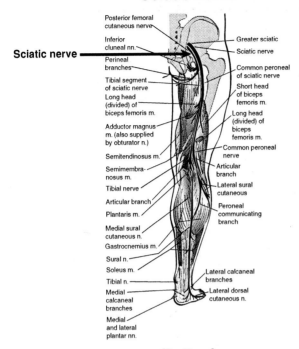

Posterior femoral cutaneous nerve

Inferior cluneal nn.

Sciatic nerve

Perineal branches

Tibial segment of sciatic nerve

Long head (divided) of biceps femoris m.

Adductor magnus m. (also supplied by obturator n.)

Semitendinosus m.

Semimembranosus m.

Tibial nerve

Articular branch

Plantaris m.

Medial sural cutaneous n.

Gastrocnemius m.

Sural n.

Soleus m.

Tibial n.

Medial calcaneal branches

Medial and lateral plantar nn.

Greater sciatic

Sciatic nerve

Common peroneal of sciatic nerve

Short head of biceps femoris m.

Long head (divided) of biceps femoris m.

Common peroneal nerve

Articular branch

Lateral sural cutaneous

Peroneal communicating branch

Lateral calcaneal branches

Lateral dorsal cutaneous n.

Buttock

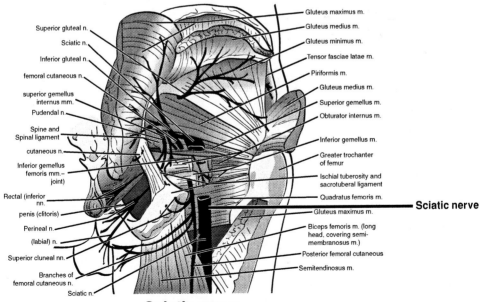

Superior gluteal n.

Sciatic n.

Inferior gluteal n.

femoral cutaneous n.

superior gemellus internus mm.

Pudendal n.

Spine and Spinal ligament

cutaneous n.

Inferior gemellus femoris mm.– joint)

Rectal (inferior nn.

penis (clitoris)

Perineal n.

(labial) n.

Superior cluneal nn.

Branches of femoral cutaneous n.

Sciatic n.

Gluteus maximus m.

Gluteus medius m.

Gluteus minimus m.

Tensor fasciae latae m.

Piriformis m.

Gluteus medius m.

Superior gemellus m.

Obturator internus m.

Inferior gemellus m.

Greater trochanter of femur

Ischial tuberosity and sacrotuberal ligament

Quadratus femoris m.

Sciatic nerve

Gluteus maximus m.

Biceps femoris m. (long head, covering semimembranosus m.)

Posterior femoral cutaneous

Semitendinosus m.

Sciatic nerve

Common Causes of Lower Back Pain

LBP has four basic causes.

Because the back is complex and is connected to the rest of the body, when you experience LBP you most likely have a mechanical problem that falls in one of four categories: muscular dysfunction pain, osteoarthritis, lumbar disc pain, or lumbar nerve root (radicular) pain.

Muscular Dysfunction Pain

When a muscle hurts, you know it. The pain stops you in your tracks. A muscle that hurts sends reflexes to the spinal cord, preventing contraction of that muscle. Thus, hurt muscles are weak. Muscle dysfunction pain is due to muscle spasm, microscopic tears, and fatigue of muscles. How does this happen?

Muscles fatigue. An example would be contracting your biceps (elbow-bending) muscle and holding it tight for a few minutes. You will develop pain in that muscle.

Poor posture and overuse can do the same thing to your back muscles. Because of the complex nature of the back, numerous structures and processes are involved in any movement; and repetition, particularly repetition of poor habits, can cause problems in many areas. Muscles do strain.

The most common cause of LBP in amateur golfers is poor stroke mechanics. The most common cause of LBP in professional golfers is overuse and fatigue. If you golf a lot, and you have poor mechanics, you obviously increase your risk. And if you are not in shape, you really increase your risk.

Many of my golfing patients who have LBP are poorly conditioned and display bad posture, and yet they are focused on their golf game. They demand Ferrari performance from their bodies, but they treat their bodies like a Yugo.

It is this mismatch that frequently leads to LBP. When the patient demands more from their body than it can reasonably deliver, muscles give out, and it hurts.

Osteoarthritis

Arthritis is a degenerative process in the joints. *Osteoarthritis* is arthritis of aging—the natural wear and tear that comes with getting older. Everyone has it, although not everyone feels it.

Some people have severe arthritis and have to live with some degree of lumbar pain. The majority of arthritis should not be painful. Often, when I review a patient's x-rays, I see what looks like severe arthritis—but when I meet the patient, they say that their back is fine and they are visiting about a shoulder problem. Pictures don't equal pain. Even severe arthritis on an x-ray does not correlate well with pain.

But arthritis is real, and it can cause pain.

Sometimes the amount of arthritis in the lumbar area is so great that there is a narrowing of the canal where the lumbar nerves exit the spine. This condition is called *lumbar spinal stenosis.*

Spinal stenosis causes pain because of the arthritis in the joints. But it also chokes nerves while you walk.

In 90 percent of cases, patients with spinal stenosis get dull aches to sharp pains down their buttocks, thighs, and legs when walking a few blocks.

In 50 percent of those with spinal stenosis, there is numbness and weakness in the legs. Patients find that the walking pain can quickly be relieved by sitting. It is walking that hurts. People with this condition often lean on their shopping carts when they walk the aisle in a grocery store. Bending at the hips opens up the canal a bit, relieving their symptoms.

Spinal stenosis, although worrisome, usually doesn't get worse. And most people who get it only have mild stenosis.

About 85 percent of all patients with spinal stenosis respond to conservative treatment. In fact, 70 percent of patients do not get worse. About 15 percent have significant improvement without surgery. Only 15 percent of those with spinal stenosis require surgery to correct the condition.

Lumbar Disc Pain

The anatomy of vertebral discs is unique.

The outer two-thirds of the disc is a tough, fibrous tissue in alternating spiral layers. This is the area where the sensation nerves of the disc are located.

The inner one-third of the disc is a gelatinous substance called *nucleus pulposis.* This gelatinous substance helps diffuse compression and bending forces.

When we age, our bodies undergo changes. This is especially true of our discs.

When we are born, our discs are 90 percent water; by the time we are 65 years old, the discs have dried to only 30 percent water. This drying out *(desiccation)* is part of the normal aging process and is not painful.

When a disc loses water, it gets shorter and wider. This is a *bulging disc.* It is a normal part of aging and is not, by nature, painful. However, tears in the outer two-thirds of the disc do occur, and these can be painful.

Most tears heal on their own in three to six months. But sometimes the tears are large and allow the gelatinous material to leak out. This condition is very painful because the jelly is irritating to nerve tissue. The leakage is the cause of nerve root pain that shoots down the leg from a herniated disc.

A herniated disc often starts with a simple, dull pop and a twinge in your back. This twinge develops into a dull backache for the next three days. After three days the back gets better, but severe pain runs from the buttock down the leg and below the knee.

Lumbar Nerve Root (Radicular) Pain

The word *radicular* means *nerve root.* The nerve root, is the part of the nerve that has branched off the spinal cord but has not yet exited the spinal canal. When this area becomes inflamed, it is called *nerve root radiculitis*—meaning the nerve is injured.

People refer to *pinched nerves* when actually the nerve is inflamed. This is the most common cause for irritation running down the leg. This inflammation is most often due to herniated lumbar discs. It shows itself as pain, weakness, and numbness.

Most of this pain can be treated successfully with time, proper posture, weight loss, exercise, anti-inflammatory injections, and physical therapy.

The healing process is slow and orderly:

- Pain goes away in 4 to 6 weeks.
- Strength returns in 6 to 12 weeks.
- Numbness goes away in 3 months to a year.

The numbness is the scariest part; but if you know it takes longer to go away, it is easier to deal with. Nerves heal slowly compared to bone or soft tissue. And the older you are, the longer all healing takes. Time, though, is on your side.

The Natural Wear of Repetitive Motion

Most causes of back pain are common to all humans. Golfers, though, put themselves at an extra risk by their choice of recreation.

Think about all you learned in this chapter about how the back works, and realize that the back must be a finely tuned machine. Now think about a golf swing and how it challenges that machine to make the same motion over and over. Muscles tire. Pressure is put on aging and wearing body parts. It is easy to fall into bad habits, and bad habits are grating on the neuromuscular system.

Golf is a great game with many rewards, but you must understand that you are challenging your body each time you swing. The best way to stand up to the challenge is to prepare yourself—read this book!

Par for the Course: A Summary

- The back is a complex instrument and is not easy to diagnose.

- Body parts wear out, but you can keep physically fit to protect against pain from wear.

- Acute pain lasts less than three weeks. Subacute pain lasts three to six weeks, and chronic pain lasts longer than three months. Most acute pain is expected to get better.

- Muscular dysfunction, osteoarthritis, lumbar disc pain, and lumbar nerve root pain are the four common causes of low back pain.

- Repetitive motion is especially hard on back muscles. Repetitive motion using poor mechanics is even worse.

Deciding to See
a Doctor

Every year, Davis Love III seems to have a flare-up of low back pain (LBP) that affects his play or sometimes takes him out of a tournament. It doesn't happen all the time, but it occurs enough to concern Love—especially because golf is his livelihood.

Given the high level of play required by the PGA tour, Love sees a doctor regularly (the same doctor who treats Fred Couples). But most people are not playing golf for thousands or millions of dollars, and you probably do not have a doctor on call.

You are playing for recreation. If pain comes, it isn't always necessary to see a doctor. Golf is not your profession.

But LBP can seem to come out of nowhere. And because LBP has many causes, it is easy for the mind to leap to conclusions—most likely, wrong conclusions.

The Mind/Body Connection

Depression is linked to pain.

The mind's ability (or lack thereof) to put life into perspective somehow translates into the body. The state of a person's mind is as good a predictor of pain as is any physical defect that appears on x-rays.

According to *Newsweek* magazine, a Canadian study "found that people who suffer from severe depression are four times more likely to develop intense or disabling neck or low back pain."

And, of course, the real danger is that LBP causes more depression, which then spirals into chronic pain and all of its effects.

Depression is not necessarily an easy thing to recognize or control. Although happiness, on its surface, is just a state of mind, it really is a state of being—and that includes your body.

The negative circle of depression and pain can be counteracted by a positive circle of exercise and relief. Functional training is not only for your body. It helps your mind as well.

Your mind and your body are not two different things. They are *you*.

Cancer

The top fear of my patients is that their LBP is cancer until proven otherwise. Although it's true that cancer can first present itself as LBP, this does not mean that LBP indicates cancer or another scary illness.

Less than one percent of LBP is caused by anything life-threatening.

Less than one percent.

Back Pain Red Flags

Most LBP is not cause to immediately run to your doctor. However, if you have certain pre-existing conditions, which I'll call *red flags*, you should visit your doctor immediately. Visit your doctor if:

- You have a past history of cancer.
- You are an IV drug user.
- You have poorly controlled diabetes mellitus.
- You have a previously diagnosed rheumatologic condition.
- You have used oral steroids for more than three months.
- You find unusual masses in your body.
- You have had recent significant trauma.

In addition, visit your doctor immediately if you have these symptoms associated with your LBP:

- Fevers, chills, and/or night sweats
- Inability to urinate; loss of control of your urine
- Numbness of your penis/vagina or anus
- Progressive weakness of one or both legs
- Progressive, unrelenting LBP not relieved by any change in positioning
- Rash or blisters involving the skin of the back or buttock
- Significant weight loss in a short period of time

Rare But Dangerous Causes of LBP

Fortunately, 99% of low back pain is not caused by anything serious or life threatening. It is unlikely that you have anything pathologic—they're very rare, and chances are the LBP slowing down your golf game is simply repetitive motion injury. However, as a responsible doctor, I need to let you know that in some rare instances LBP can indicate a more serious problem:

- Inflammatory disorders (such as rheumatoid arthritis)
- Hormone and metabolic disorders or changes (such as Paget's disease of the bone)
- Infections (such as a disc infection, herpes zoster, or shingles)
- Tumors (benign or malignant cancer)
- Visceral (organ) referred pain (such as a kidney infection)

These are a few of the reasons you must pay attention to red flags in LBP.

Pain Without Red Flags

Most acute LBP flare-ups are caused by a muscle strain or by irritation of an arthritic joint in the spine. These acute flare-ups can usually be treated with a short period of rest, ice or heat, and a few days of taking things slowly.

For muscle spasms, inflammation of the joints of the spine, or inflammation of the nerves of the lumbar spine, the best medications to start with are found over the counter. Ibuprofen and Naproxen are over-the-counter Non-Steroidal Anti-Inflammatory Medications (NSAIDs).

A general plan is to take NSAIDs at full strength (as indicated) daily for one to two weeks. But the general plan doesn't work for everyone.

When should you go to a doctor for your LBP? There's no black and white answer, although I'll remind you again that most LBP heals on its own without any treatment.

However, here are some general guidelines. See a doctor if:

- You have severe acute LBP and you have rested for two days, but you are still unable to get out of bed due to the pain.

- The pain is severe enough to drastically reduce your activities (for example, you can't go to work) and is not getting better after five days.

- You have severe, burning pain shooting down your leg, and NSAIDs don't work. Most likely you need stronger anti-inflammatory medications than are available over the counter.

- You have *any* new loss of sensation or weakness of your legs.

- You have *any* incontinence of your bladder or bowel.

- You are not comfortable starting an exercise program on your own. A physician can give you a prescription to see a physical therapist who can help you learn exercises that help.

Imaging Studies: "Doc, I want an MRI"

In art and in life, a picture is worth a thousand words.

In medicine, a picture doesn't always tell a clear story. It's the oddest thing, but the lack of correlation between what is found on images and what patients say they feel is profound.

A medical picture sometimes means nothing other than, "Gosh, look at that." It's true. Most pictures mean nothing when compared to symptoms. However, many patients today think doctors can diagnose anything by using modern imaging techniques. One of the most popular is the Magnetic Resonance Image (MRI). An MRI machine uses a very strong magnet to create a detailed black-and-white picture of a specific area of your body. Unfortunately, a black and white photo of your body's anatomy does not adequately explain what may be going on in the body. For instance, a picture of your spine will not tell the doctor if there is subtle inflammation of those tissues, nor will it demonstrate if a nerve is angry (painful) or not. As an example, check out the following sets of statistics:

Existence of Bulging Disc in People *Without* LBP

Age	Occurrence
30–39	32%
40–49	65%
50–59	82%

It turns out that disc bulges are a normal part of aging. They mostly indicate you are getting older, and that's it. When we are born our lumbar discs are made of 90% water. This water makes our disc plump and bright on an MRI scan. By the time we reach the age of 65, our discs are only made up of 30% water. With this drying out, the disc becomes a bit shorter and wider; the disc also appears darker on an MRI. The widening of the discs creates the disc bulge.

A herniated disc is different from a bulging disc. A herniated disc occurs when a tear of the tough outer layer of the vertebral discs allows the *nucleus pulposis* (a jelly-like material in the disc's center) to leak outside the disc. This material can be very irritating to nerve tissue and is a major cause of nerve pain. A herniated disc can also be large enough to actually compress (or pinch) a nerve. However, not all herniated discs are painful.

Up to 30 percent of the patients report no pain, even when their MRI clearly shows a herniated disc.

Existence of Herniated Discs in People *Without* LBP

Age	Occurrence
20–29	15%
30–39	21%
40–59	30%

It makes sense to order a test only if it can help direct and change treatment. So, before I ever think of ordering an MRI, I get the patient's history and do a clinical examination. Doctors in my position have seen enough patients over time to be able to figure out what is happening in many cases.

However, sometimes a physical examination and a look at the patient's history do not reveal clues. That's when I turn to the imaging studies.

I order an MRI for these reasons only:

- If a patient has four weeks or more (after treatment) of nerve-type pain shooting down the leg with or without sensory loss or weakness. Generally, this type of pain responds to treatment within four weeks. If it lasts longer than four weeks, the patient may need lumbar surgery. The MRI would be ordered for a surgeon, to give a general picture of the area before surgery. It is a sort of pre-surgical imaging study (MRI is not a procedure).

- A patient's history and physical examination suggest spinal stenosis. An MRI is ordered to evaluate the stenosis. This also is a sort of pre-surgical imaging study.

- When red flags are present. In this case, the MRI is to rule out possible pathological causes for LBP.

- I need more information to find out what is going on with someone.

So, don't panic if your doctor doesn't order an MRI. These kinds of expensive imaging tests don't answer all questions; and chances are, the doctor already has a pretty good idea what's causing your LBP.

Par for the Course: A Summary

- The mind and body are connected, and depression is often linked to LBP.

- Less than one percent of LBP is caused by a life-threatening problem.

- There are red flag history indicators as well as symptoms that should lead you to see a physician immediately.
- Most acute flare-ups go away on their own.
- Doctors can help in certain situations.
- Imaging studies are not usually necessary.

Finding the Right Treatment

L ow back pain (LBP) can be frightening, but it usually does not have frightening causes.

As you learned in Chapter 2, when the frightening causes are ruled out, treatments can focus on the mechanical aspects of the low back. What I mean by *mechanical* is the physical components of your back: the muscles, lumbar vertebrae, tendons, ligaments, discs, nerves, and joints and the way they all work together.

The problem with treating LBP is that there is often no one thing that goes wrong. Many things can go wrong, and each is so different that there is, in turn, no one particular treatment.

There are many answers.

One thing is certain: Pain does not always mean tissue injury. Sometimes, it's just pain. LBP is difficult to diagnose, and there are many answers. Within all the answers exists an incremental approach to treatment, and within this approach is an essential foundation of *exercise*.

The standard non-operative treatment plan for athletes consists of these eight steps:

- Stop the inflammation.
- Restore flexibility.
- Restore strength.
- Restore aerobic conditioning.
- Restore balance and coordination.
- Adapt the rehabilitation program to sport-specific training and exercises.
- Start slowly back into the sport.
- Return to full function.

Dealing with inflammation, and even surgical approaches, will be considered later in this chapter. It is important, though, to remember that your body is your most important ally. (A full program of exercise is explained in Chapter 8.)

The Cornerstone: Exercise

No matter what the problem is, the cornerstone treatment for LBP is exercise. Your body needs exercise—it leads to less pain, less anxiety, and less depression, and it promotes weight loss.

Even if LBP forces you to stop activity for a couple of days, do not give up the idea of getting back to your normal life.

Yes, sometimes you need rest, but you never need a lot—two days at the most. Once you have given your body a chance to rest and recover, it is time to start moving again.

How do you know what to do, and how much to do?

The best answer is to listen to your own body. You know your capabilities better than any doctor ever will. You know what you *can* handle. And, you must realize that you really can handle exercise.

If you don't have a clue how to begin, the best thing is to just go for a brisk walk.

The key is to do something called *normalizing*. Normalization means getting back to your normal daily activities as soon as possible. This way you do not develop poor, guarded movement patterns.

Normalizing has its foundation in the fact that activity is safe and activity is good. The closer you can come to doing what you used to do, the closer you *are* to doing what you used to do. It's a circular argument that makes perfect sense because your body needs exercise.

Your body reacts to your habits, and exercise is a good habit. Although physiological changes (or an accident) beyond your control affect how you feel, there is a lot that you can control.

People need exercise. It is part of any treatment. But some patients may not be able to start an exercise program right away. They may need physical therapy first.

Physical Therapy

Some patients may not be able to jump into an exercise program. They may need help making the connection between their brain, their back muscles, and their abdominal muscles. Physical therapy performs this function by helping you relearn how to use your body.

Physical therapy is a low-level exercise program for injured or out-of-shape bodies. It is individualized. It is coached. And it is challenging. The idea of physical therapy is to challenge your body and to teach yourself to find those physical connections between mind and body.

Physical therapy can involve many different ways of stimulating muscles—from low-level electricity to the use of demanding equipment such as balance balls. Physical therapy is often done in conjunction with the use of medication to reduce inflammation and control pain.

Medications

If your low back hurts, medicine can help. Medications are used to control inflammation and to reduce pain. And they do work.

A thorough discussion of the medicines used to treat LBP is beyond the scope of this book, but here is a short list of medications commonly used to treat LBP.

Non-Steroidal Anti-Inflammatory Drugs (NSAIDs)

NSAIDs are a class of drugs designed to decrease inflammation and help control pain. They are common medications—available in prescription strength and over-the-counter (OTC) strength and used for musculoskeletal pain. You'll recognize some of the familiar names, such as Motrin, Aleve, Advil and Ibubrofen (the same thing), Relafen, Lodine, Feldine, and so on.

NSAIDs are a class of medication that controls pain, inflammation, and high temperature in the body; they work by decreasing chemicals in your body called "prostaglandins." NSAIDs work best when taken at the prescribed hour, around the clock, for a length of time ranging from few days to a few weeks. They all work basically the same way, although you may want to try different types because they are made of slightly different chemical compounds.

Warning: NSAIDSs are potent medications that can cause side effects including gastrointestinal upset, allergic reactions, high blood pressure, dizziness, confusion, and bleeding of the gastrointestinal tract. It is best to take medications with food. Consult your physician if you take these medications for more than four straight weeks.

Muscle Relaxants

Muscle relaxants do not specifically relax any muscles; they are sedatives. Commonly used muscle relaxants are Flexeril, Robaxin, Skelaxin, and Baclofen. They are only available in prescription strength.

Muscle relaxants work in the spinal cord and the brain, and essentially they knock you out. The relaxation of muscles is a secondary reaction to the drug's primary purpose as a sedative. These medicines also help patients sleep.

> **Warning:** Muscle relaxants can be abused. I limit their usage to two or three days if possible.

Oral Steroids

Oral steroids are the strongest drugs that reduce inflammation to control pain. Only available as a prescription, they are used when patients have lumbar pain running down to the thighs and legs. Nerve injury is caused by an inflammatory process, and oral steroids work to reduce inflammation. They are very potent, but they are safe if taken for a short period of time.

> **Warning:** Taking oral steroids for a long period of time is dangerous. They can give you cataracts, affect your blood cells, give you diabetes, thin your skin, thin your bones, cause you to gain weight, and burn a hole in your stomach.

Narcotics

Narcotics are pain relievers, also known as *analgesics*. Some commonly used narcotics include Vicodin, Tylenol #3, Darvocet, Percocet, Morphine, Dilaudid, Oxycontin, and the Duragesic patch. They are only available by prescription.

These medications work best when taken at the prescribed hour around the clock. They do not work best when taken "as needed." The main goal of narcotics is to control pain so that patients can increase their activity level and normalize their motion. These drugs can be used safely.

> **Warning:** Addiction is rare. This is part of the warning with narcotics, because patients are sometimes worried more about addiction than they are about treating their pain. True addiction means depending on the drug for something other than its intended use. Yes, narcotics can be addictive. But their intended use is to help reduce pain.

Anti-depressants and Anti-seizure Drugs

Anti-depressants and anti-seizure drugs are used as part of a whole-body approach to treatment, and they help control nerve pain. Both are types of prescription drugs. Antidepressants include drugs such as Prozac, Paxil, Pamelor, and Elavil. Some antiseizure drugs include Neurontin and Topamax.

It is not exactly known how these medications help block pain, but they do reduce the excitability of nerves in the spinal cord. Plus, they can be part of the approach of healing the mind to help motivate the person to work to heal the body.

Injection Therapy

In some cases, it is best to target the medicine at a specific place by using an injection.

Most injections use steroids, because steroids are effective at reducing inflammation. Targeting pain by injecting steroids is more direct than taking oral steroids and simply getting the medicine into the bloodstream.

The most common injections are as follows:

- *Epidural steroid injections/transforaminal injections* for nerve inflammation due to herniated discs or due to arthritis. These injections are given in the epidural space—between the bones and ligaments of your spine. This space is only 5 millimeters wide, and an injection at that spot gets right to the nerve. This treatment may include up to three injections, given weeks apart.

- *Facet steroid injections* into the joints of the spine—called facets—to calm the pain of arthritis.

- *Sacroiliac joint injections* given for inflammation of the sacroiliac joints of the pelvis.

- *Radiofrequency ablation (destruction)* of select painful nerves or nerves that give sensation to painful structures. These are last resort injections.

- *Myofascial trigger point injections* to help break up muscle spasms and to stretch out chronically tight muscles.

Intradiscal Electrothermal Therapy (IDET) and Nucleoplasty

Disc pain sometimes does not respond to conservative treatment. In certain cases, Intradiscal Electrothermal Therapy (IDET) and Nucleoplasty can work.

This procedure, performed by medical subspecialists, is used to control painful discs. A wire, or catheter, is fed into the outer portion of the disc and is then heated to destroy the fine nerve endings of the disc. It is also thought that the procedure causes some changes in the architecture of the fibers that make up the disc, thus helping to control the pain emanating from the disc.

This is a new procedure. The longest anyone has been followed after the procedure is only three years. So far, these procedures seem to have about a 70 to 80 percent success rate in controlling pain from the lumbar discs. The long-term effects are still unknown.

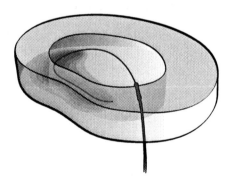

IDET: A wire is inserted in the disc and heated to control pain caused by the lumbar disc.

Research

A 2002 study of 58 IDET/Nucleoplasty patients by Jeffrey Saal, MD, and Joel Saal, MD, in the medical journal *Spine* showed that about three-quarters of patients experienced a reduction of their pain. There were no complications, adverse effects, or worsening of pain at the two-year follow-up visit.

Another study of 80 IDET/Nucleoplasty patients at the Walter Reed Army Medical Center showed a success rate (success is defined as a greater than 50 percent decrease in LBP) of 50 percent. It also found that patients who were obese had only a 10 percent success rate with the procedure.

Patients must meet a few requirements in order to qualify for this procedure:

- They must have at least 50 percent of their disc's height left. This is one time when an MRI is very handy.
- They have experienced LBP for more than six months and have not experienced satisfactory improvement with non-operative care.
- They have already tried and failed with a nerve-block procedure such as an epidural injection.
- They have had a normal neurological exam.
- They experience LBP with very little leg involvement in the pain.

Finally, before IDET/Nucleoplasty is performed, patients undergo a procedure called a *discogram*. This procedure determines if the lumbar disc is really the cause of LBP. During a discogram, a needle is inserted into the lumbar disc; then, under low pressure, dye is pumped into the disc. The dye shows up on x-rays and can reveal cracks or fissures in the disc material. In addition, if the disc is the problem, the dye introduced into the disc will reproduce the pain the patient is experiencing.

Warning: IDET/Nucleoplasty is not a risk-free procedure. Damage to the nerve or disc can occur. Complications are rare, but this treatment should only be considered after more conservative options have failed.

Surgery

Surgery is a last resort. As I tell my patients, "Do not change your God-given anatomy unless you have to." When do you have to? Rarely. You should only consider surgery if you have any of the following problems:

- Progressive weakness and numbness of one or both legs due to a herniated disc or spinal stenosis.
- Any loss of bowel or bladder function (incontinence).
- Herniated lumbar disc with nerve inflammation that has failed conservative treatment for more than six weeks.
- Pathological cause for LBP such as a tumor, an unstable fracture, a cyst pushing on a nerve, and so on.

Sometimes surgery is appropriate for LBP. However, 99 percent of LBP and sciatic distribution pain *does not require surgery*. In addition, 85 to 90 percent of herniated discs will heal without the need for surgery.

Studies have shown that surgery for herniated discs is not necessarily more helpful than conservative treatment. Surgical patients initially do better (in the first couple of years) than non-surgical patients, but non-surgical patients do better after ten years.

I just can't say it enough: Surgery is a *last resort*.

The most common surgery for damaged or diseased discs is disc removal followed by spinal fusion. *Spinal fusion* permanently connects the bones of your spine together. This is done using either a piece of your pelvic bone or metal plates and screws. Spinal fusion can cause problems—including pain at the site of donated pelvic bone, loosening of metal plates or screws, false joints forming in the spine, and degeneration of the discs above and below the site of the fusion.

Prosthetic Discs and Larry's Story

The FDA approved disc replacement surgery in October 2004. The surgery involves the complete removal of a lumbar disc. This disc is replaced with an artificial disc made of metal and plastic.

In studies, prosthetic discs seem to be safe and have shown satisfactory results in reducing LBP for patients whose pain was caused by their disc.

Unlike spinal fusion, disc replacement surgery aims at maintaining the physical characteristics—including range of motion and spreading of forces—of the disc being replaced. However, disc replacement surgery should never be a first option. All surgery is risky, and often it is unnecessary. For instance, consider the story of my patient, Larry.

Shortly before the FDA approved prosthetic disc surgery, Larry came to see me about his long history of LBP. He knew that he had degenerative changes in his lower lumbar spine. He had dealt with this chronic pain for years, and he was able to function.

Larry came to me because he had developed a deep burning sensation in his right leg. The pain was constant throughout the day.

At the time, Larry was 65 years old; and, among other things, he had money to burn. I mention his money because Larry, unknown to me, was also researching prosthetic disc surgery, which was already legal in Germany.

In my evaluation of Larry, I told him there was a good chance that his pain was coming from his back. I also told him that there could be other causes. I recommended a full work-up, including x-rays, an MRI of his spine, and a series of blood work. I also recommended a nerve test for his right leg.

Well, that's when Larry's money took over. He was looking for a quick fix. Instead of showing up for his tests, he went to Germany. He spent $30,000 to have two prosthetic discs put into his back, because he was convinced he knew the cause of his problem.

Three months after his operation, Larry returned to my office. He told me his pain had not gone away.

Larry told me that he wasted a lot of money. I agreed.

So, finally, we proceeded with the original plan of testing and discovered that Larry had a neurological condition called multifocal sensory neuropathy—a disease of the nerves. It is caused by the autoimmune system.

Larry's leg pain had nothing to do with his back.

The point is that surgery should be a last resort. First, give your body a chance to heal itself; and second, make sure you are attacking the real problem. Just ask Larry.

Par for the Course: A Summary

- The cornerstone of all treatment for LBP is exercise.
- Medications are most helpful when they are used to relieve pain so that you can begin exercising.
- Medications work best when taken as prescribed.
- Treatments such as injection therapy and Intradiscal Electrothermal Therapy (IDET)/Nucleoplasty can be effective, but they should be considered only after more conservative treatments have failed.
- Surgery should be a last resort.

Part

The Game of Golf

Examining Why Golfers Get Low Back Pain

While playing in the Western Open in Chicago on June 27, 1975, Lee Trevino was struck by lightning and subsequently hospitalized. Although he kept playing that year, he later developed back pain, and the next year he needed surgery.

Most causes of back pain in golfers are not quite so dramatic.

Because golf is a game of the torso, the back undergoes tremendous repetitive stress due to continual twisting in one direction. All motion sports such as javelin throwing and baseball put stress on an athlete's back, but golf, as a sport for all ages, is particularly stressful—especially for those who have not taken the time to strengthen the muscle support around the spine.

A Quick Glance at the Golf Swing

The cascade of events that occur from the time you address the ball until you finish your swing is awe-inspiring. Everything happens very fast; and as the neuromuscular chain of events unfolds, a body that is not fine-tuned may make instantaneous adjustments to compensate for any lack of conditioning.

In other words, your body is smart. It knows what it can and cannot do, and when you challenge it to do something that it isn't ready for—take a golf swing with a poorly conditioned back, for instance—it makes changes in this intricate movement. And these adjustments, made to stop pain, may actually make things worse. Doing something wrong, and doing it repetitively, is a recipe for injury.

When a well-conditioned athlete steps up to the ball and begins to swing, the brain first thinks about moving. As it does, it automatically sends a signal down the spinal cord to the transverse abdominis muscle, and before you even move, the transverse abdominis muscle immediately tightens up to protect the back. This is truly an amazing function. However, an out-of-shape golfer loses this function and the protection it provides.

Of course, more than one muscle is involved. The interconnection of muscles, nerves, bones, and joints that function as your core (explained further in Chapter 7) act as a unit.

Golfers often concentrate on their arms and hands for club control or on their hips and legs for power. But in reality, the most important muscles are those in your core that connect your upper body to your lower body.

Studies show that professional golfers can activate their abdominal muscles twice as quickly as amateurs can. This, much like the skill involved in actually playing the game, comes from correct training. Quite simply, athleticism—and especially your golf swing—starts in your core.

The Four Causes of Back Pain in Golfers

As I mentioned earlier, golf is a game of the torso, and the repetitive twisting—especially in one direction—is hard on the back.

When your core is in shape, it takes much of the pressure off your discs. All golfers experience some compression in their spine as they swing, but those who have a conditioned core end up with much less compression.

A study published in the *Journal of Manual and Manipulative Therapy* showed that golfers with low back pain (LBP) have a reduced ability to maintain a static contraction of their abdominal muscles. In addition, this study demonstrated that golfers without LBP were able to use their abdominal muscles more on their downswing than could golfers who suffered from LBP. When core muscles are easily fatigued, causing muscle dysfunction, the load of a golf swing is transferred elsewhere—to the spine.

Those who have a strong core have built up a sort of shock absorber system for their spine. Yet even professional golfers get LBP.

Golf injuries can be narrowed to four major causes, following the mnemonic CATS:

- Change—Change in your grip, swing, equipment, or frequency of play can lead to injuries.
- Alignment—Swing mechanics play a role in low back health.
- Twisting—The rotation of a golf swing can wear down poorly tuned back muscles.
- Speed—The faster you swing, the more stress you put on your back, and the greater your risk of injury.

How Change Can Cause Injuries

Overuse injuries may be the most prevalent type related to change. Golfers may take a golf vacation, or the weather may change, or any variety of other reasons may occur that increase the frequency of golfing. The golf swing is already stressful, and when the frequency of playing increases, so does the frequency of injuries.

But change can mean any new way of playing. Changing your grip or your swing, for instance, can *change* how your body reacts during a golf swing.

Even changing equipment is enough of an alteration to possibly cause injury. This means that any time you undergo a change in your game, you are putting your body at risk.

How Alignment Can Cause Injuries

Recreational golfers injure themselves most often because of technical deficiencies in their swing. Poor swing mechanics used over and over—an average of 50 times on an 18-hole course, or 300 times in a practice session on the driving range—can cause damage to soft tissues.

Injured golfers tend to take fewer lessons than those who are not injured. A study in the *Journal of Sports Medicine* showed that golfers with LBP had considerably less bend in their low backs (seven degrees) than golfers without LBP (25 degrees). This measurement was obtained by subtracting the curve of the spine when addressing the ball from the curve of the spine during the downswing. Essentially, golfers with LBP have a decreased range of motion of their lumbar spines.

Injured golfers most often are those who follow the time-honored technique of the true amateur—the grip-it-and-rip-it gang, pushing their inflexible backs to the extreme end of motion, thus causing pain. This means that poor technique can cause injury. It also means that golf lessons can help more than just your score.

How Twisting Can Cause Injuries

The golf swing comprises a multilevel system using the club, arms, shoulders, torso, hips, and legs rotated around the axis of the spine to generate maximum club speed. This rotation stresses the system that makes your back work. *Everything* is stressed by the twisting.

Players with fitness deficiencies—in flexibility, strength, or balance—tend to overload the lumbar and abdominal musculature during a swing. Those who start without a proper warm-up are also at risk, because the body is not ready for the twists of a swing. This can all lead to muscle fatigue and/or muscle compensation for the deficiencies in your swing, and ultimately to injury.

Fatigued muscles lose their shock-absorbing ability and stress the spinal discs and joints—leading to pain. If your back is tired after a day of golfing, you are at risk for injury from twisting.

How Speed Can Cause Injuries

The faster you drive an automobile, the greater your chance of having an accident. This rule also applies to golf and other athletic activities.

In golf, a club can reach 100 miles an hour in .02 seconds. This incredible acceleration asks a lot of your body. Yet in every round of golf that you play, you try this dozens of times. And the faster you move, the greater the danger of injury.

Your automobile insurance company knows about this risk. It increases premiums for every speeding ticket. Your doctor knows about it, too. The physics of trying for quick acceleration is an equation that tests your body's limits. And when your body is not in shape, those limits are a lot lower than when you have taken up functional training.

The Vicious Circle

It is common for the body to try to compensate for pain. When a repetitive activity such as a golf swing seems to be the cause of your hurt, you unconsciously make changes in your swing to lessen the pain.

THE PRINCIPLE

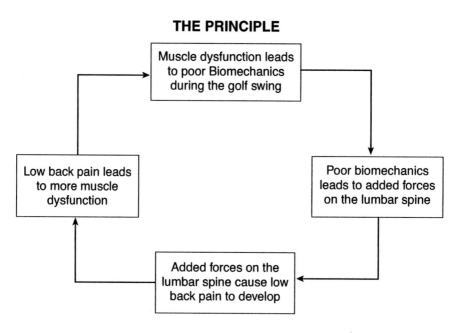

A vicious cycle of muscle dysfunction, leading to LBP

The goal of this book is to help you decrease the forces on the lumbar spine by improving the biomechanics of your golf swing through correcting trunk muscle dysfunction. Correcting this muscle dysfunction will not only improve your golf swing but will also prevent this vicious cycle of events from happening.

The problem, of course, is that when you do make such changes, they can exacerbate the problem. But the circle can be even worse if you give in to the pain. For instance, if you take time off work because of back pain, you will find yourself on a slippery slope. The longer you stay away from any activity, the harder it is to get back into it.

Someone sitting home all day can easily let pain fill time so that it becomes a reason for living. Every physician has patients who feel they need their pain. The doctor visits and the struggle against pain are all the person has in life. It's sad, and often the patient realizes the futility of such an existence, but they continue on this path because they feel that they have nothing else.

Some patients end up in bed and become so fearful of any movement that they do less and less. Then, when they move, they end up walking like a soldier, stiff and in block movements. This behavior, just like a bad golf swing, leads to the development of bad movement patterns, causing muscles that are not being used to atrophy. So the cycle continues.

Anyone who resorts to bed rest for a week—even a great athlete—loses 10 to 15 percent of muscle mass in that one week, because muscles atrophy quickly. Five weeks of bed rest result in a 50 percent loss of muscle mass. At that point, the cycle can seem inescapable. But there is a way out.

Comparing Golfers With and Without LBP

Anyone who ever saw Jack Nicklaus at his best knows how well he played when he did not have LBP. He won 18 major championships on the way to a professional golf career that many consider the greatest of all time. In 2002, however, Nicklaus played in only two Champions Tour events because of persistent LBP.

Comparing golfers with and without LBP can sometimes amount to comparing different stages of life, as witnessed by Jack Nicklaus. Although age is certainly a major variable between golfers with and without LBP, other factors come into play as well.

Here are some common characteristics of golfers with LBP:

- They tend to have a poor range of motion of their lumbar spines.

- Their abdominal muscles tire more quickly than those of golfers without LBP.

- They bend their lumbar spines to the left or to the right during the golf swing approximately 80 percent of the time.

- They bend at the lumbar spine and not their waist/hips while addressing the ball.

Golfers *without* LBP also share some common characteristics:

- They are able to use their abdominal muscles more on the downswing when compared to golfers with low back pain.

- They demonstrate more than twice as much trunk velocity (speed) on the downswing generated by increased abdominal muscle activity.

- They have a greater ability to hold their abdominal muscles in a state of contraction (activation) than golfers with low back pain.

Perhaps the most obvious difference between the two groups, as witnessed by the need for this book, is physical conditioning. Golfers who have LBP often have poor core conditioning so that the body's natural shock absorbers—a tremendous function when it works—are worn down, leading to bone-on-bone friction. LBP in golfers is often the results of poor abdominal conditioning, causing the body to compensate in ways that, quite simply, lead to pain.

Abdominal muscles contribute most of the power generation for the acceleration in the backswing. Because abdominal muscles fatigue more quickly than back muscles—especially in individuals with chronic LBP—the body compensates by recruiting the muscles of the back to do the work. Again, the body is smart and can make adjustments when the right muscles aren't ready. But this inappropriate muscle recruitment increases the likelihood of developing injuries to the low back.

Often, fundamental differences exist between golfers with and without LBP, especially in regards to swing mechanics. It is well documented in pain literature that patients with LBP have a decreased range of motion of their lumbar spine. And yet the range of motion of the lumbar spine is a key element in the power needed in a golf swing. Golfers with LBP still try to rotate as much as golfers without LBP, thus causing stress on the structure of the lumbar spine and, in effect, making the pain worse.

A study in *Clinics in Sports Medicine* showed that during a golf swing using proper swing mechanics, downward loads (compression) experienced by the lumbar spine are eight times that of your body weight. In other words, take your body weight and multiply it by eight, and you know how much weight you are applying to your back every time you swing a club. This study also showed that spinal compression was 1.5 times greater for amateur golfers than for professional golfers and that poor swing mechanics of amateur golfers accounted for much of this extra load. The study concluded that amateurs often swung harder, trying to get acceptable distance.

If your mechanics are off, you put larger loads on your lumbar spine, and those loads grow even more if you swing harder. It's another vicious cycle, proving again the importance of strengthening your core and learning good swing mechanics to take as much pressure off your spine as possible.

Richard's Story

Richard is a typical golfer in that he is always tinkering with his swing, trying to make it better. Although he is by no means a professional golfer, golf nevertheless gives a lot of meaning to his life—it takes him away from the doldrums of his 9-to-5 job.

One day, when he discovered how a little "C" curve in his left side during his backswing improved his distance, he did the natural thing. He kept doing it. And his tinkering, indeed, added a bit of consistent power to his game, so he kept doing it. He loves golf, and he improved, so he loved his new swing.

But about the same time, he developed a daily constant dull ache in the center of his back, with some pain radiating to his left buttock. When Richard went to his family care physician, he was sent to a back class. There he learned about the workings of the back. This was good, but his pain remained.

An MRI was ordered, and it revealed some minor wear of his lumbar discs, but it wasn't unusual for a middle-aged man such as Richard. In fact, the changes in his lumbar spine were certainly present before the onset of his pain. But his family physician told Richard that his LBP was probably from "bulging discs" and recommended that Richard adopt a sedentary lifestyle and stop playing golf. To Richard's credit, this advice was unacceptable, and he asked to be sent to a pain specialist.

When Richard came to our department of physical medicine and rehabilitation, he was convinced by one of my colleagues to try prescription-strength anti-inflammatory medication for six weeks along with physical therapy for several one-on-one treatment sessions. Still, his pain remained. Depression about his condition began to get to Richard, and his golf game seemed to exacerbate both his pain and his depression.

His first bit of luck hit when he met a physician's assistant (Clare) in my office for a second opinion. Upon evaluating his history—especially the fact that he felt worse during and after he played golf, but not after other physical activity—Clare thought Richard might have a golf-related injury. She referred Richard to me.

By the time Richard came to see me, his frustration about his pain and his lack of response to treatment was palpable. We started talking about his golf game, and I found that the beginning of his pain coincided with a change he made in his swing.

He demonstrated his swing for me. I saw, and he explained, the "C" bend and the reason for it. This small side bend caused a misalignment that prevented his body from rotating around the vertebral column. Repetitive swings caused repetitive stress and caused the pain.

He entered the vicious cycle—he adopted guarded posturing that allowed the muscles of his back to become tight and dysfunctional, and he developed chronic daily pain. So, he gave up the activities that he loved. And that made his physical and mental conditions—always linked—worse.

This side-bending stuff appeared logical from the patient's perspective and yet very ill-advised to me—a brand new golfer and a doctor dealing in back pain. I, as a new golfer, wanted more power. Richard did have more power, so that seemed like good logic. But in this case, Richard's new power came at a high cost. In the end, Richard's cost for more power turned out to be no power. He hurt too much to play golf.

At first, the change made him happy because it added power to his game. Until his visit with me, he hadn't noticed that the change to his game coincided with the beginning of his low back problems.

As I evaluated his pain and his golf swing, the link became obvious. Richard returned to a proper alignment for his golf swing, but disappointment roiled his face because he had convinced himself that he would lose power. We talked.

We talked about functional training.

We discussed how distance lost from the change in his swing could be replaced by a change in his technique. Richard went on the program. By strengthening and improving the function of the muscles in his low back, he increased the power in his swing and was shooting longer distances in no time. Three times a week he performed the exercises, and he spent other days at the driving range perfecting his pre-"C"-curve swing.

Eight weeks later, Richard returned to my office. He smiled, offered me tickets to the Buick Open, and said with astonishment, "I can't believe that part of my treatment is to play golf—okay, play golf the right way—and that it works."

Par for the Course: A Summary

- Swinging the wrong way and repetitively is a recipe for injury.
- Golf injuries fall in four categories under the mnemonic CATS—Change, Alignment, Twisting, Speed.
- The vicious cycle of a bad swing causing pain is often followed by a worse cycle of pain causing bed rest, causing even more pain.
- Core muscles are important in golf because they connect your upper body to your lower body, they power your swing, and they protect your spine.
- Swing mechanics are an important part of having a healthy back for golf. Thus, golf lessons help more than just your score.

Analyzing the Golf Swing in Pieces

Until a year ago, I didn't golf. Instead, my athletic endeavors tended toward more intense activities such as triathlons, snowboarding, mountain biking, in-line skating, and mountain climbing. To better prepare for these activities, I discovered the wonders of functional training. With functional training I was performing strengthening exercises where groups of muscles worked together in concert so that I could become a better athlete.

The first time I went golfing was because one of my interns, who once played amateur golf with Tiger Woods, said the game might appeal to me. When it did, I was amazed. But more astonishing than the fact that I actually liked golf was my discovery that the muscles groups I was focusing on in my functional training program were the exact same ones used in a golf swing.

This chapter analyzes the golf swing in a way it has never been looked at before—with a focus on the muscles used in each part of the swing. A proper swing should decrease the stress placed on the body and therefore reduce or prevent injury. Of course, a proper swing also helps your score.

Here, the swing is broken down into six parts based on significant muscle interactions and not on instructional methods (using a right-handed swing model):

- Start and take away
- The move halfway back
- Taking it to the top
- Powering down
- Completing the release
- Finish

1. Start and Take Away

The first phase of the golf swing is addressing the ball. The set-up posture is crucial for the proper positioning of the swing—from your take away on through your impact and to the finish. The set-up posture should consist of a stable base formed from relatively equal distribution of weight from the heel to toe of each foot. Too much weight on the toes places stress on the front aspect of the knees (kneecap joints), which are more prone to repetitive stress injuries. The feet should be roughly shoulder width apart, with equal weight distribution. As for aiming, if you draw an imaginary line from the front of your back foot to the front of your front foot, the line should continue directly to your target. This position may vary from club to club and for specific shots, but it is used here for simplification. The legs and hips should feel as though you are squatting as if to sit down.

The start

The squat position activates the muscles of the quadriceps, buttock, hamstrings, and abdomen. A proper squat thus distributes the weight evenly over the lower body, decreasing pressure on the low back. The back and neck are flexed only slightly in this position. The upper body is bent forward at the hips instead of at the lumbar spine. Bending at the lumbar spine causes stress and strain on the lumbar spinal musculature and puts your spinal elements at great mechanical risk. Most of my patients who have back strain and/or herniated lumbar discs have bent and twisted at the same time. These injuries can happen without any lifting involved, such as in a golf swing. The key to addressing the ball is to keep your back as straight as possible during the backswing so that twisting of the lumbar spine occurs only during the backswing.

In this posture, the abdominal muscles should be engaged, taking stress off the low (lumbar) back. Weak abdominal muscles can put all the weight of the upper body on the low (lumbar) back, creating strain before the swing even begins. Your arms should be relaxed and should hang down, gripping the club in a comfortable position.

Addressing the ball

A common error is gripping the club too tightly and tensing the forearms at address. Holding the club too tightly prevents proper positioning throughout the swing. One of the main differences between beginning and advanced golfers is the smoothness of their swings. A tight grip does not allow other larger muscles to participate and leads to a forced swing. The key to a good golf swing and prevention of injury is balance and fluidity. A golfer in the proper position forms a stable base to withstand a relatively forceful push from the front. A golfer in the proper position remains balanced. Improper positioning at address puts extra stresses on the low back throughout the swing.

The take away involves a very coordinated move between the shoulders and the arms, working together as a unit. An imaginary line drawn between the two shoulders and lines from each shoulder to the hands reveal the famous *triangle.* This triangle should be maintained as the club begins its path away from the ball. This is achieved by allowing the large muscles of the chest (pectoralis major), shoulder (deltoids), and back (latissimus dorsi) to contract. The club head should remain outside of the plane created by the hands during this initial move. Although it is a simple move, it is one of the most important and the source of proper position at the top.

As the club leaves its starting position, it should follow a ball-to-target path until the body rotation begins. The final part of this initial move preserves the triangle, which now is formed with the hands at the right hip. A common error during this move is using the wrists or arms to force the club away from the ball. This usually results in the club going inside the ball-to-target path too quickly, leading to poor position at the top. This also causes a collapse of the triangle formed at address. The poor positioning at the beginning puts added stress on the other back muscles around the spine (paraspinals) and back joints (facets) later in the swing to bring the club back into position.

The take away

2. The Move Halfway Back

As the shoulders and arms, acting as a unit, reach the right hip, the unit moves through the "hand off" position to the cocking of the wrists. The *hand off* position refers to the point where the club is parallel to the ground and could be potentially handed to someone standing to the golfer's side. In order to achieve this position, the golfer should feel the left arm extend outward. The hips and legs begin their movement shortly after the take away has started. The hips shift a couple of inches toward the right by the time the club is in the handoff position.

From here, the right arm continues to fold, and the lower body (legs and hips) and the upper body (shoulders) continue their rotation. The club is brought through this handoff position, and the wrists are allowed to cock. This position results in the left arm being relatively parallel to the ground and the club placement being approximately perpendicular, 90 degrees, to the ground from a head-on view. A key element is the preservation of the plane formed by the club at address. The angle created by the spine at address also remains unchanged. Taking the club off this imaginary plane places the club in an unbalanced position that the body must eventually compensate for.

Moving halfway back

The move halfway back

3. Taking It to the Top

From the 90-degree angle created by the wrist cock, the club moves to the top of the swing parallel to the ground and roughly pointing toward the target. The shoulders end in a position 90 degrees from address with the back facing the target, and the hips take a final position 45 degrees from address. The left arm should be allowed to bend at the shoulder at the top. At this point, a majority of the weight has moved to the right side, distributed evenly across the right foot. The left heel may lift slightly.

Taking it to the top

The back angle is still preserved, and the head should not move up and down. From address, the body has moved a couple of inches from left to right to allow for the weight transfer and coil. Once again, the stable base from front to back should be preserved. An imbalance of low back and abdominal musculature can lead to a loss of the back angle created at address. If this occurs, the back must be forced back into position during the downswing to make contact with the ball. From a head-on position, in this situation, the head appears to bob up and down during the transition at the top. It is a natural tendency, especially if you have a previously injured back, to stand up slightly at the top of the swing. This bob up and down puts a tremendous amount of compressive force through the low back discs and facets.

A common error seen at the top is over-rotation, resulting in the club pointing to the right of the target and moving past parallel. This can occur if the club is brought inside of the swing plane, forcing increased rotation in the back to get the club to the top. A fast backswing can bring the club past parallel and may even result in some weight transfer to the left side. The back must make a large adjustment in this position to get the club back on the proper path. This places a lot of stress on the left lumbar spinal joints and overstretches the lumbar spinal musculature.

On the other hand, some golfers, due to structural limitations of their spines, may not be able to bring the club to parallel at the top. In this case, the rest of the elements should be preserved, and a comfortable position at the top should be the goal.

The top

The top: a side view

This rotation, from halfway back to the top, incorporates the arms, shoulders, torso, hips, and knees to create a tight coil of the body that stores power for maximum club-head acceleration at impact. Shoulder motion is especially utilized to generate more torque in the lumbar region. The rotator cuff muscle of the right shoulder is the kingpin of this shoulder rotation. This coiling of the body is the key for generating distance for your golf game. Another way of thinking about the power of uncoiling is from a different sport, baseball. A Major League Baseball pitcher uses every inch of his body to get a baseball over the plate at blazing speeds. The difference between a pitcher uncoiling his entire body and a person throwing from the elbow (the old cliché, throwing like a girl) is enormous. The inefficiency of throwing from the elbow leads to a maximum distance of only 20 feet or so, whereas a top-conditioned pitcher using his entire body can throw the ball 90 feet at 90mph or more. The body, when it stores energy and then uncoils, can do amazing things.

4. Powering Down

From the top of the swing, the built-up potential energy is allowed to unwind in an orchestrated sequence of events. A slight movement toward the target by the left leg is the first motion, followed by the left hip. This movement from the lower body leads the arms and right shoulder to fall into the correct position and keeps the club on the proper plane. The left leg moves into a stable position as the hips unwind to the left. The abdominal muscles provide much of the rotational strength while the back (paraspinal) muscles provide support. The arms guide the club on the same plane, formed at address, where the butt end of the club points toward the ball. In this position, the body and club are in correct position for the release.

Powering down

The key to the power-down movement is the role of the left leg and hip as the initiators of the downswing. After initiation, *the abdominal muscles become the power generators.* The abdominal muscles contract before any other trunk muscle and before the arm musculature. As the abdominal muscles contract, other muscles join in to maximize acceleration of the swing. The muscles of the buttocks, the thighs, and the low back are activated as well as the chest muscles (pectoralis major) and the rotator cuff muscle of the shoulder.

During powering down the torso muscles unwind.

To develop maximum acceleration in the downswing phase, the golfer activates a *stretch reflex* principle. By stretching the abdominal muscles to the right during the backswing, the muscles essentially snap back to the left like a rubber band. Here, the strength and flexibility of the abdominal muscles are important. This is why the further a person can rotate his or her shoulders away from the target during the backswing (rotational capacity), the greater the clubhead speed, and the further that golf ball will fly.

This trunk rotational capacity is the most important lever in achieving maximum speed during the golf swing. Players who are technically less skilled or who are older have up to 50 percent less trunk rotational capacity than younger players or individuals who have excellent technical skill.

It has been found that twice as many back injuries occur during the downswing as occur during the backswing. This is easy to believe given that during the downswing, the club covers the same range of motion as the backswing but twice as fast. Remember, speed is a risk factor for injury.

Flexibility and strength of the trunk musculature are the most important variables for performance and the most important determinants for the risk of injuries.

A swing from the top by the hands or the arms prematurely unwinds the coil, resulting in a complete loss of the stored potential energy. A swing from the top also results in a congested position of the hands, arms, hips, and legs at impact, causing loss of accuracy and power. It also puts the body in a position where multiple compensations are necessary just to make contact. Once again, this type of error causes stress throughout the body and severely weakens impact power.

The abdominal muscles become the power generators.

5. Completing the Release

Once the left hip has rotated through and the arms are brought down into proper position, the release is ready to begin. The release consists of a rapid movement of the right and left arms, working in coordination to bring the club back to address position. The shaft of the club at impact is tilted forward, and the left wrist is straight. The left leg and hips have already cleared the way for the release and are open (facing left of the target) at impact. The transfer of weight during the downswing results in much of the weight being on the left side at impact, with the right knee moving toward the target line. The club continues through the ball, staying close to the ground and continuing along the swing plane.

Completing the release

This overall movement creates a whip-like action as the right arm turns over (pronates) through impact. The power at impact is attributed to clubhead speed secondary to rotational capacity. The speed and force with which the club head releases is largely dependent on flexibility and muscular strength providing power and stability. It becomes obvious how an imbalance of muscular strength and decreased flexibility can lead to injuries, given the force created during a swing. During ball impact, the golf swing produces a significant degree of back side-bending to the right. This can be uncomfortable for those individuals with significant right-sided arthritis of the spine.

It is also important to mention that at the moment of ball impact, the forces on the left leg and the left hip, exerted from the weight transfer to the left side, become significant. Thus repetition of weight shift can provoke a risk of injuries and discomfort in the hip area, particularly for older players with hip arthritis.

From a performance standpoint, the purpose of the impact is to hit the ball as far as possible in the proper direction. From a safety standpoint, the purpose of the impact is to have a smooth transition from acceleration to deceleration.

Ball impact   Start of follow through

6. The Finish

The finish is characterized by a progressive *deceleration* of the club. About 25 percent of all golf-swing injuries occur during the finish phase. The danger for injuries of the lumbar spine arises if the deceleration of the club occurs too quickly. The momentum of the golf club pushes through halted musculature, leading to small tears of the muscles.

The momentum of the release carries the club through as the arms guide it into a comfortable finishing position. The right leg follows the right hip and faces the target. The right foot comes off the ground and rests on the toes. The body should be vertical, and the back should be in a neutral (natural) position by the rotation of the body around the axis of the spine. The momentum of the swing should bring the golfer into this position with little force, allowing the large muscles of the shoulders (deltoids), chest (pectoral), and back to naturally decelerate and guide the club into position.

The body rotates around the spine.

Middle follow through

Right shoulder is lower than the left. The spine is straight.

Attempting to force through the finish can result in the back being over-extended backward, absorbing the shock. It can also lead to over-rotation, putting further stress on the joints of the back. These positions leave the golfer in an uncomfortable finishing position with compression forces through the back. Forcing the follow-through can also over-rotate the spine, causing rotational stress. These errors result in the golfer falling away from the target to catch his or her balance. A proper finish often results in the golfer taking a step forward. You should be able to keep a balanced finishing position without discomfort. Although some of these subtle errors in swing mechanics may not instantly result in injury, they start a process in which damage accumulates.

The finish

Par for the Course: A Summary

- The set-up posture should consist of a stable base formed by relatively equal distribution of weight from heel to toe of each foot.

- Don't hold the club too tight. Doing so prevents proper positioning throughout your swing.

- An imaginary line drawn between the two shoulders and the lines from each shoulder to your hands reveals the famous triangle. This triangle should be maintained from the beginning of the swing.

- The key to powering down is the role of the left leg and hip as the initiators of the downswing.

- After initiation of the downswing by your left leg and hip, your abdominal muscles become your power generators.

- Flexibility and strength of your trunk musculature are the most important variables for performance and the most important determinant for the risk of injury.

Part

The Program

Examining How Muscles and Nerves Work

A complicated cascade of events takes place before you start any movement, including a golf swing.

It begins with electrical impulses emanating from the motor control area of the brain into special nerve fibers running from your brain into your spinal cord. From there, these electrical signals follow nerves that sprout off the spinal cord into your muscles. And then the muscles spring into action.

Sometimes you think about it. Sometimes you don't.

Your body includes two systems, and they work in concert. In one of the systems, you think about and plan your action. In the other system, things are done for you automatically.

The Autonomic Nervous System

Your body is equipped with a system that controls muscles and has them do things without you ever thinking about it. This is called the *autonomic nervous system.*

Perhaps the easiest example to understand of this system at work is the use of muscles when you digest food. Many muscles are involved in your digestive system, and yet you don't think about digesting food. Your body does it for you.

Your body, with your autonomic nerves, does many things for you. This system is used in all of your actions, because even in actions that you control, stabilization is required.

The autonomic nerves branch off the spinal cord in much the same way as nerves that control voluntary movements. The nerves travel to the muscle, where they attach to special fibers within the belly of the muscle. These are called *muscle spindle fibers.*

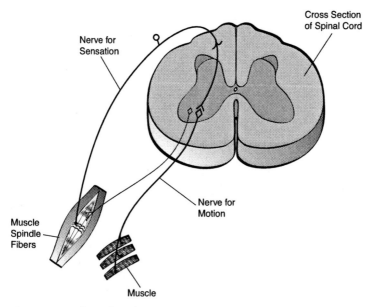

Cross section of spinal cord

How the Spinal Cord Works

Muscle spindle fibers within the body of the muscle send sensory information to the spinal cord. This sensory information is used by the spinal cord to adjust the contraction (tone) of the muscle. The information travels from the spinal cord to the muscle via the motor nerve.

The muscle spindle fibers act as control centers of the muscle, communicating with the muscle and telling it how to move when you are not actively communicating with the muscle.

As I've said, your body does a lot of things for you while you are busy not thinking about it. Your reflexes, for instance, are part of your autonomic nervous system. Your muscles are, in theory, always ready to react. Even when you are resting or sleeping, your muscles are in a slight state of contraction. This is called muscle tone.

You can see muscle tone, or lack of it, by looking in the mirror. Muscles have a shape to them. When you look at an athlete or a body builder, you see distinct muscle tone. But muscle tone provides you with more than just a nice-looking body.

Good muscle tone allows your muscles to function at their best through reflex action. Reflex action works when the muscle communicates with the spinal cord about the way it is being stretched. A reflex impulse travels to the spinal cord, and the impulse is sent back to the muscle to accommodate that stretch in some way.

Reflex Action and Programming

Your body is naturally equipped with reflexes. For example, if you are about to fall, you automatically stick out your hand to catch yourself. Reflexes are part of almost any action as your autonomic nervous system works in tune with your conscious efforts. Reflexes work best from toned muscles that have been trained to deal with challenges. When muscles are not used, they atrophy; and when reflex muscles lose their effectiveness, the rest of the body suffers.

The body is always programming itself according to its daily habits. If those habits are to do nothing, then muscles and muscle reflexes may not respond when they are eventually challenged.

If you want to golf, you really challenge your reflexes. The precise and powerful movement required by a golf swing is especially vulnerable to deficiencies in your reflexes.

When you program your body, you input signals into your brain about to how to do something properly (or improperly); over time, your brain and your muscles begin to recognize that pattern. If you challenge your body now, your body will respond to challenges later.

The Role of Your Core Muscles

As you know, muscles go in various directions across your abdomen, and each of them plays a role in stabilization. What is interesting is that each of these core muscles has two connections with nerves. A connection between a muscle and a nerve is called an *innervation*.

Because muscles in the abdomen have two innervations, these muscles can partition and perform different tasks. This is helpful because these muscles have so many different functions.

Thus, training these muscles is essential. A lot is going on in that one area of your body, and it needs your attention.

Tired Muscles

Injuries happen at many different times, but I have noticed that they usually happen when athletes have reached their edge of fitness and become fatigued. In other words, tired athletes injure themselves more often than athletes whose bodies have not yet been worn down by their particular sport.

For instance, skiers tend to hurt themselves on the last run of the day. Golfers also end up getting hurt more often on the back nine than on the front nine. Why? Because fatigued muscles lose their protective reflexes and become more fragile. This is where sports injuries often start.

The best way to prevent injury is to prepare your muscles in advance. Muscles with increased endurance, strength, and flexibility are much less apt to become injured. That is why it is important to prepare your muscles ahead of time with a fitness program that gets you ready for the activities you plan—such as 18 holes.

Balance Training and Proprioception

An amazing trait of your body is your ability to recognize where your joints are in space, time, and angular velocity. That is called *proprioception.*

Try this: Close your eyes, and move your foot up and down. You feel it moving, and you know where it is without looking at it. That is proprioception.

Over time, humans have lost some of our proprioception abilities, especially our ability to handle uneven surfaces. We are so used to pavement and flat shoes that natural terrain is difficult to navigate. I visited an art show in Austria in which the artist put an uneven floor of rocks and divots into the room. It was difficult to walk on, and the feeling reminded us of how we have lost some of our balance abilities.

Although we have lost some of our proprioception skills, you can improve your personal feeling. There are dynamic exercises (see Chapter 9) that incorporate balance, angular velocity, and groups of muscles working in concert. As your body does the inner choreography programmed by these exercises, it trains itself to be ready to react to challenging situations.

The most sensitive muscles of reflex action are those in your torso. These muscles create a cylinder around your spine and are the target of functional training.

Functional training is designed to increase the tone and reflex activity of this muscle cylinder around your spine. When you increase the strength of your torso muscle cylinder, you increase the effectiveness of this cylinder at taking weight off your spine. And when you do that, you can move more freely and without pain.

No one walks around actively contracting abdominal and back muscles. We rely on reflex tone to do the job for us. The great thing is that you can train your reflexes.

Par for the Course: A Summary

- Muscles at rest are ready to spring into action.

- Nerves connect to muscles, sending signals from your brain.

- Some muscles can partition themselves, performing two tasks at once.

- Your autonomic nervous system, which controls muscles such as reflexes without you thinking about it, can be improved with training.

- The muscles around your spine create a cylinder that acts as a shock absorber.

Back Basics: Posture and Body Mechanics

Life is about habits, and no habit pertaining to your low back is more important than your posture. The way you carry your body and your mechanics of doing things have a great impact on how you feel.

Every day, you do the same things. These everyday life patterns set your muscles into habits; they then either help keep your body in working order or are responsible for things breaking down. Most of what you do is not neutral with regard to your health. It either helps or hurts.

The things you do every day affect how you feel. In the big picture, you certainly know the benefits of exercise and the risks of, say, smoking cigarettes. But your body also reacts to the habits of posture.

You train your body by living. Although it may seem silly to even examine the basics of posture, doing so is actually very smart because posture is the most basic part of conditioning your back. And practice makes for good body mechanics.

Sitting

How do you sit?

Quit laughing—this is a serious question.

Think about this: It is easy to slouch. And for some reason, our brains have conditioned us to think that the slouching position is the most comfortable. It can certainly fool us into thinking it really is comfortable, except that the comfort it brings is full of consequences.

Slouching can hurt you.

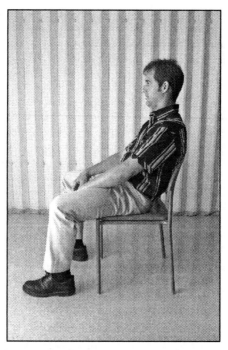

Slouch sitting leads to back pain

The main point is to sit back and upright. If you have a straight-backed chair that does not encourage a curve in your back, you have to encourage it on your own. A neutral curve in your back is important to minimize stress to your spine. Put both feet on the floor, and sit back.

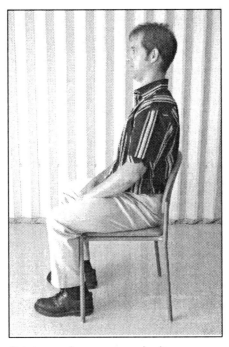

Sitting properly protects your back

It's also easy to encourage your natural curve while sitting. Use a pillow. Or, find a different chair that encourages proper posture.

If your chair is the seat in your car, you may first get in and think it is comfortable. Car seats are designed for comfort. However, they are not necessarily designed for good posture, so you may find it necessary to use a lumbar pillow—a pillow behind your back can help maintain a little arch so that you can sit without having to actively work.

Finally, when you are sitting, shift positions occasionally. Even the best posture, when continued for more than 30 minutes of sitting, can cause increased pressure on your back. Just don't slouch.

Standing

Slumping while standing equates to slouching while sitting.

It might seem like a good idea until it becomes a habit. When you slump, you don't maintain the natural curve in your back, and therefore all your muscles must work harder.

When standing for a length of time, try instead to stand on one foot and kick the other slightly behind you so that you balance the toes of that foot on the ground. This little adjustment instigates muscles in your low back to contract and helps you maintain the standing position.

Little things help a lot. For instance, try swaying slightly when standing. Just go from one foot to the other and back, as fast or as slow as you want. This motion varies the pressure on your muscles so that you are not stuck in one posture and stressing one muscle.

One final trick is to put one foot on something slightly elevated in front of you. Think of the metal bar with a footrest that runs below the barstools at your favorite restaurant. Those footrests are for the people who are standing as much as for those who are sitting.

Use the same theory when standing at a kitchen sink. Open the cupboard in front of you, and put one foot inside. Or get a book, and slightly elevate your front foot. This little action activates muscles that help you maintain a standing position.

Resting

During rest or while lying in bed, it's not essential to maintain the curve in your back, so for most people, lying on your side is fine. A pillow, of course, is needed to support your head.

If you want, a pillow between your knees can help keep your hips in a neutral position while sleeping. (Plus, it keeps your knees from knocking together.)

Lying on your stomach tends to be a good position for your low back. Unfortunately, it may create a problem for your neck.

So, extra pillows can help. Some people sleep with a sort of body pillow so that they are lying between their side and their stomach. The pillow is between their legs; it can also support the upper arm.

Should I get a new bed?

A good bed can, in a few select cases, help ease back pain. But solving the problem with a bed is a rare exception. A firmer, supportive mattress is best. If you sleep on your back on a very soft mattress, and the mattress creates a big reverse curve in your back, the result will not be good. The slump position is bad, even when you are sleeping.

Standing from a Chair

We often overlook how simple things in our daily lives, when done improperly, can lead to low back pain. Just leaning forward to get out of a chair puts a lot of stress on your back, and the cumulative pressure throughout the day adds up. To reduce the mechanical stress on your low back when rising from a chair, follow these simple guidelines. As an added bonus, every time you get out of a chair properly, you are strengthening your legs. Do that many times a day, every day, and you can relieve a lot of strain from your back as well as increase leg strength.

To learn how to stand from a chair properly, begin with a good sitting posture. Sit back, and maintain that natural curve in your back. Now, instead of leaning forward at the waist, scoot your butt forward to the edge of the chair.

Moving your rear to the edge of the chair puts your body closer to your feet. Your feet are underneath you. Now, *use your legs* (not your back!) to raise your body. Think of this movement as a leg exercise.

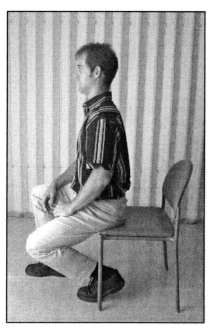
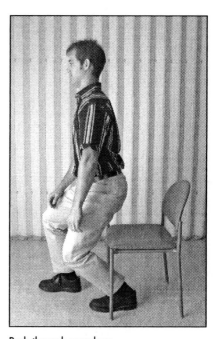

Move to the front of the chair   Push through your legs

Getting Out of Bed

It is not the best idea to throw yourself out of bed, using torque and twisting. Instead, if you are lying on your back, roll to your side, toward the edge of the bed, and drop your feet to the floor. Next, use your arms to push into a sitting position.

Any preventive technique, especially on creaky waking muscles, is an opportunity to take stress off your back.

Lifting

It is common for people to hurt their backs while lifting objects. The reason is poor mechanics.

Mechanics are simple, as long as you understand three basic principles:

Principle 1: Face the object. Your feet should face the object, and your body and shoulders should be square to the object.

Principle 2: Get on the level of the object. For example, if an object is down low, you need to bend your knees. You can kneel down to one knee, or you can squat down, but the idea is to get to the object's level. If the object is up high, get a stepladder and boost yourself to the level of the object.

Principle 3: Bring the object close to your body. The further away an object is from your body as you lift, the harder it is to lift.

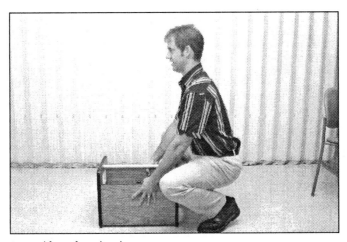

Proper lifting: face the object

Bring the object close to your body

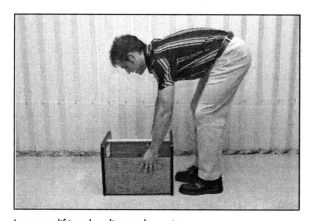

Improper lifting: bending at the waist

Dishes

Taking dishes out of a dishwasher can be the kind of repetitive chore that causes problems. The common way is to grab dishes and then stand and twist while putting the dishes in their place on the shelf.

Instead, try kneeling down on one leg and stacking a few dishes on the counter. Then stand and face the dishes, and put them up on the shelf.

Groceries

Putting groceries into and taking groceries out of a car trunk is a natural way to cause unnatural twisting. Grocery carts don't line up with trunks. And groceries don't stay close to the edge of trunks. Leaning in and bending to pull up groceries can cause problems. Instead, try pulling groceries close to the edge of the trunk before lifting them. When you are lifting groceries from a cart, keep your nose and butt aligned, and keep the groceries close to your body—especially in any transfer to another location.

Jaffe's Law

Lifting? Do not bend and twist.

Lifting is simple. Follow Jaffe's Law: Keep your nose and your butt in the same plane.

Improper lifting: Do not bend and twist at the same time

Standing at a Sink Shaving or Brushing Your Teeth

You do not have to have your head right over the sink when you are shaving or brushing your teeth. No law says you must. A better way is to stand back, away from the sink.

If you are brushing your teeth and you need to spit, don't bend at the waist. Instead, bend at the knees to be closer to the sink. The same with shaving and rinsing out the razor.

It is more important to take care of your back than it is to worry about being too close to the sink or to the mirror.

The Golfer's Lift

To pick up small objects, such as a golf ball, you can use a technique that can be handy on and off the golf course. Some golfers use a golf club as support for one arm while they bend at the waist to pick up a ball. The idea is to hold onto the club and let one leg stay straight out behind as they bend.

You don't have to use a golf club to support you when you bend. You can use anything, such as the arm of a chair.

The golfer's lift

Par for the Course: A Summary

- The physical effects from the habits of posture are cumulative. Everything you do adds to how you feel.

- When sitting, sit back and maintain your natural curve. Consider using a lumbar pillow.

- When standing, put one foot in front of you or behind you, and shift positions frequently.

- When changing positions (for example, sitting to standing), practice proper body mechanics every time.

- When lifting, keep your nose and your butt in the same plane.

Get Ready: Getting Started and Finding the Correct Equipment

U nless you are ready, you are not ready. That sounds funny, but it is true because a stagnant body needs to prepare for activity. Neuro-energy follows thought, and you have to learn to make that connection. You also need the correct equipment on hand when you start. Get ready.

Even if you have been stagnant, it's time to challenge yourself. Get ready.

Preparing should be a short routine, the same every time. Get your body together. Get your equipment together. And then...

The order of exercise follows a simple formula:

- Flexibility

- Muscle balance

- Stability

- Strength

- Power

Challenge yourself. That's the idea.

Restoring flexibility and balance are the foundational steps to any exercise program.

Functional training requires maintenance of your center of gravity over your base of support. That's a challenge. These exercises are more taxing on your body and require more concentration and coordination than simple free-weight or machine-based exercises.

As a result, exercise order needs to also be taken into consideration. Exercises should progress from the most to the least complex. The nervous system takes longer to recover from an exercise than the musculature system.

That is why you should always start with those exercises that are the most challenging for you or the ones that require the most balance. You do this because the body is most ready for the challenge at the beginning of your exercise.

The next phase is to train and condition the stabilizers of the body. Building on the foundation of a now balanced and stable body, strength training can begin.

Finally, after the body is balanced, stable, and strong, power or high-speed training can be implemented with a minimal chance of injury.

For those with severe LBP, the initial steps may be difficult.

Physical Therapy for Some

If when starting this program you develop steadily increasing muscle pain for more than one week, this is a signal that you may need to begin with *physical therapy* before embarking on a *physical training* program.

Physical therapy is performed by a licensed practitioner who works with the physical aspects of a medical illness. Physical training is considered weightlifting to condition muscles for improved strength and movement.

Individuals with severe LBP may need to see a physical therapist for specialty training before basic strength training can begin. Physical therapists can identify structural abnormalities and educate you on proper posture and positioning. Therapists can also start the important process of getting you in touch with your core muscles. Some individuals have very poor proprioception (the ability to know where your joints are in time, space, and angular velocity—for example, the ability to move your foot without looking at it). Some individuals have such poor coordination that they do not know how to feel their musculature.

Therapists, starting with very subtle movements, can train individuals to feel the muscles that need to be strengthened. Neuro-energy follows thought.

You must be able to feel a muscle and move it in isolation before it can be strengthened in conjunction with other muscle groups. A physical therapist can help you do this.

The First Connection

Before you start a functional training program, you need to make the connection between your mind and your abdominal muscles. Here is a simple exercise that you can perform to make that connection.

Get on your hands and knees. Your arms should be straight down from your shoulders. Your thighs should be straight down from your hips. Now, take a big breath in, and push your stomach out a bit. Hold this position for one second.

Breath in and stomach out

Next, pull your abdomen into your spine while breathing out. You should be able to feel your abdominal muscles tightening. When all the air is out of your lungs hold that position for one second. Practice this breathing exercise for a couple of minutes every day for one week. Soon you will feel very comfortable contracting your abdominal muscles correctly.

Breath out and stomach in

Home or Gym?

Exercises like the one described above can be performed at your own home or at a gym.

Everyone is different, and everyone's home gym and workout space is different. But I generally prefer that my patients go to a gym, because that way they make a time commitment. A gym also surrounds you with a healthy workout environment, so people usually work a little harder than they do at home. Plus, a good gym provides a professional staff to help with form and technique.

Group Exercise

Groups are good for exercise consistency.

Group exercise is the type of fun, friendly environment that can encourage you to show up again—and that, more than anything, is why groups are good. Groups encourage you to exercise.

I think that aerobic, muscle sculpting, and Pilates classes taught by certified instructors help push you a little harder than you might on your own. Plus, the instructor is there to make sure you are doing the exercises correctly.

And, of course, the socializing that goes along with group exercise is a bonus. It is easier to make a commitment to go to a class when you know a group of individuals you will see week after week.

Which Gym?

Almost every city and town has more than one gym. Which gym should you join?

The answer is simple: Join the gym closest to your house or work. If you limit the hassle factor with transportation, you will be more likely to go to the gym. Join the gym you will actually exercise in.

Machines to Use

Only two of the exercises listed in this program require a gym weight machine. If you prefer to work out at home, you can skip these two exercises in the program. If you are working out in a gym, the two machines I recommend you use are the Lat Pull Machine and Cable Rack Machine.

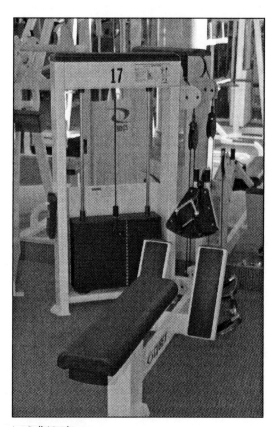

Lat Pull Machine

Cable Rack Machine

Equipment Anyone Can Afford

The rest of the exercises can be performed with simple and inexpensive exercise tools that you can purchase for the home.

● **Burst resistant exercise ball:** Ball sizing is as follows:

Individuals 5'2"–5'8" use a 55cm ball.
Individuals 5'9"–6'2" use a 65cm ball.
Individuals 6'2" and over use a 75cm ball.

These balls usually run from $25 to $60.

● **Basic balance board or 20" rocker board:** These boards run from $40 to $70.

● **Soft medicine balls:** These are nonbouncing, soft-shelled weight balls. I recommend 4lb. to 10 lb. medicine balls. These balls usually cost $30 to $60.

● **Dumbbells:** I recommend dumbbells from 5 to 25lbs. There is a large price range, from $40 to $200.

Burst resistant exercise ball

Basic balance board

Rocker board

Soft-shell weight balls

Dumbbells

All this equipment can be purchased at any sporting goods store. These products are also available over the Internet; I recommend a company that specializes in exercise equipment for functional training called Fitter International Inc. (Calgary, Alberta, Canada; fitter1.com).

Because I have become a golfer and seem to treat a great many patients whose LBP is attributed to golf, I have related my functional training to this sport. However, these exercises are applicable to anyone suffering with LBP from repetitive motion.

Par for the Course: A Summary

- Preparing for exercise is important. Get your body ready, and get the right equipment.

- Exercise follows a formula of going from the most challenging, while your body is fresh, to the least challenging.

- Some people need physical therapy to prepare their body for an exercise program. Physical therapy gets the mind in touch with your core muscles.

- Most exercises in the program can be done in your home or a gym, but a gym usually provides more incentive to work out on a regular schedule.

- Most equipment can be purchased for a nominal cost. The real payment you make is a commitment to stick with it. And this payment pays off.

Using Functional Training to Change Your Life

To show the importance of fitness to golf, two mobile fitness centers—48-foot trailers full of equipment and trainers—park at every PGA and Senior PGA event. One look at this generation of athletic golfers such as Tiger Woods and Annika Sorenstam shows that fitness training is as important as practice on the putting green for those who play professional golf.

In many ways, fitness training is even more important for amateur golfers, and the best fitness training in the world is functional training—exercises that emphasize movement patterns rather than just strengthening individual muscles.

The Basics of Movement and Functional Training

Neuromuscular movement is the communication between your brain, your spinal cord, your peripheral nerves, and all of your muscles so that your body is working as a unit. The three areas of neuromuscular development as they relate to a golf swing or any activity are as follows:

- *Stabilization*—Being able to go into a slight squat position and maintain that position as you maintain your range of motion of a golf swing.

- *Locomotor motion*—Being able to move your body, as in a golf swing.

- *Manipulative movement*—Manipulating an outside object, such as a golf club.

A golf swing requires stabilization so that you can use locomotion in order to manipulate a golf club. All the elements are important in a golf swing, and so functional training works on all three areas.

When you use traditional gym equipment, you isolate a muscle so that the body's built-in stabilizers do not need to work. Functional training changes the formula so that you are challenging the body's stabilizers to a higher degree than you might normally encounter in any endeavor, and you are training the body to work as a unit.

The Program

The program is a set of functional training exercises for core strengthening. Based on a regime that emphasizes movement patterns over isolated muscle groups, the functional training exercises in this chapter utilize the body's own *righting and tilting reflexes* so that you will develop better balance and flow of your physical activity.

These exercises incorporate many balance and rotational movements with a focus on the muscles of the pelvis and shoulder regions.

Functional training for core strengthening

The Science of Squatology

The most fundamental exercise in core strengthening is the squat.

Proper squatting technique strengthens your abdominal muscles (especially transversus abdominis), the quadriceps, the hamstrings, and the postural muscle of the back. These are the key muscles in your golf game—the muscles giving the most support to your lumbar spine. Proper squatting technique teaches you balance through your body's center of gravity. This center of gravity lies about an inch in front of your sacral bone (what you think of as your tailbone). Proper squatting technique also prevents knee pain with exercise by shifting your weight away from the vulnerable front portion of your knees.

Learning how to squat correctly takes patience and practice. It takes time, so spend at least a week learning how to squat before venturing further with this exercise program.

Technique makes all the difference.

The Proper Squat

There are lots of ways to do a squat incorrectly. Here you'll learn how to perform this exercise for maximum strength and efficiency.

- *Hold a Medicine ball or dumbbell* at chest height and about 6 to 12 inches from your body. Your feet should be about a shoulder width apart. Your toes should face forward. If necessary, you can angle your toes outward up to 30 degrees for comfort.

- *Fold at your back and hips* into a seated position. Think of your butt being in the back of an imaginary seat.

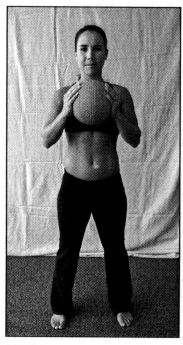

Step 1   Step 2

● *Your weight should go through your heels.* (You should be able to wiggle your toes.) Your shins should be perpendicular to the ground, and make sure that you do not shift your weight to the right or to the left. Stay centered.

Step 3

● There should be a nice curve in your back.

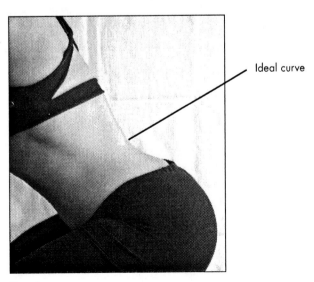

Ideal curve

Step 4

- Squat down, *holding your lower abdominal muscles tight* by pulling your belly button in toward your spine. Hold that position all the way through the exercise. Your knees should be just over your toes with your chest up.

- Push up through your heels, and extend your hips through your buttocks muscles. Perform 10 to 12 repetitions for 4 sets.

Step 5

Step 6

Advanced Squat

The advanced squat uses a barbell bar, allowing you to utilize heavier weights to increase your strength.

- Start with the 45lb bar until you get the form down, and then add weight slowly.

Step 1

● Remember to keep your butt in the back seat and your weight through your heels.

Step 2

Reverse Lunge

The reverse lunge stretches and strengthens the muscles of the abdomen and hip region. The lunge also encourages opposite sides of the body to work together in a coordinated movement.

- Balance on your *left* leg. Bring your *right* leg up to 90 degrees.
- Hold 5 to 10lb weights up just below your ears. Take some practice runs without the weights.

Step 1

- Lunge your *right* leg back slowly so that your right knee almost touches the floor. Take two full seconds for this motion.
- At the same time your *right* leg is lunging backward, raise your *left* arm above your head.

Knee should not be in front of the toes.

Knee should almost touch the floor.

Step 2. Side view

Step 2. Front view

- Bring your *right* leg up to 90 degrees again (take two seconds), and bring your left arm back down to neutral.

Step 3

- After a set of 10, switch leg and arm for another set of 10. Perform for a total of 3 sets of 10 repetitions, alternating each leg.

To challenge yourself, place an unsteady surface under your stance foot, such as a soft mat or a balance board. If you are having trouble with this exercise, start with your feet together. Try a reverse lunge, and bring your feet back together. Try that with your other leg. This exercise can also be done without moving your arms until your balance improves.

Single-Leg Driver Lift

This exercise is a mainstay for core strengthening. The single-leg driver requires balance and activates the larger core muscle groups.

- Your weight should be on your *right* leg. Put your hands out in front of you with the thumbs up. Extend your *left* leg back with your *toes pointed down.*

Step 4

- Bend your *right* knee, and extend your left *leg* back (by contracting your butt muscle). Go as low as you can.

Step 2

- Rise up to the position from step 1. Repeat 8 times on each leg for a total of 3 sets.

Step 3

Hamstring Curls

For this exercise you need a floor mat and large resistance ball.

● As a starting position, lie on your back with your heels up on an exercise ball.

Step 1

● Lift your butt up off the mat so that your body is straight. This may take some practice for balance.

Step 2

- Bring the ball toward you, *keeping your back straight*. As you get stronger, try it with one leg.

Step 3

- Perform 8 repetitions for a total of 3 sets.

For a more advanced exercise, lift one leg up off the ball.

Step 4

Prone Pitching Wedge

The prone pitching wedge is a wonderful back strengthening exercise.

- Start in a push-up position with only your *feet on the ball*. For proper alignment, please note the three points of contact with the wood dowel: *butt, mid-back,* and *back of the head.*

Step 1

- Pull the ball toward you by using your legs. Keep the same alignment.

Step 2

● Extend your legs to the starting position. Perform this exercise for 8 repetitions, for a total of 3 sets.

The Divot Maker

The Divot Maker is a functional training exercise specific for the game of golf. For this exercise you need a cable machine set high up. Use 20 lbs to 60 lbs.

● Grab the cable with *your arms straight.* Assume a semi-squat stance.

Always keep your arms straight.

70% of your weight should be on your inside foot.

Step 1

● Pull the cable across your chest, *keeping your arms straight.* (You will feel the tension most in your arm closest to the weights) Bend your outside knee, and shift your weight to the left. Rotate your inside leg/foot if that feels more comfortable.

Rotate foot toward your hands.

70% of your weight should now be on your outside foot.

Step 2

- Don't take a lot of breaks with this one. Perform 10 repetitions on one side, and then turn and face the other direction to do 10 repetitions on the other side. Perform 3 sets.

Reverse Divot Maker

The Reverse Divot Maker requires more strength because you are working more against gravity.

- Start with the cable at its lowest setting, with the same amount of weight as in the Divot Maker or slightly less weight. Keep your arms straight.

Start in a partial
squat position.

Step 1

- Pull the cable up across your chest, bending the outside knee. Here, too, rotate your inside foot toward your hands.

Step 2

- Perform 10 repetitions on one side, and then turn and face the other direction. Do 10 repetitions on the other side. Perform 3 sets. Do this exercise right after the Divot Maker exercise.

Mulligan Twist

The Mulligan Twist adds rotational flexibility to your spine. Start this exercise slowly with your knees bent. Work within your comfort level.

- Get on your back, and extend your arms anchored by two weights. Extend your legs up to the ceiling as best you can. (This will vary depending on your flexibility.)

- Rotate your waist to one side. Then rotate your waist to the other side.

Step 1

You can bend your knees at 90 degrees to make this exercise easier.

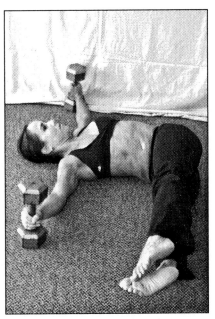

Step 2

- Perform 3 sets of 10 repetitions. If your back hurts, try this exercise with your knees bent at 90 degrees.

Abdominal Crunches

This exercise is second only to the squat in its importance to your program.

Your abdominal muscles are the most important muscles to strengthen in order to unload and protect your spine. These muscles create a cylinder around your lumbar spine to protect it. The abdominal muscles are also the first to start working in your golf swing. They are the initiating muscles in the complex combination of events that form a perfect swing.

There are four abdominal muscle groups: rectus abdominis, external abdominal obliques, internal abdominal obliques, and transversus abdominis (your innermost abdominal muscle). To maximize the efficacy of your abdominal musculature, the transversus abdominis needs to contract first and then send a signal to the other abdominal muscles to contract in sequence. The exercises in this program are designed to get your transversus abdominis to work before your other muscles.

- Lie with your back on an exercise ball and your hands up to your ears but not supporting the back of your head.

If you cannot bring your head all the way back, that's OK.

Step 1

● *Pull your navel toward your spine,* and begin to roll upward starting from your head to your neck to your torso.

Step 2

● Finish when you can no longer roll up any farther without lifting yourself off the ball. Your abdominal muscles should feel fully contracted.

Step 3

- Reverse the rolling (now going from your low back to your head) slowly.

Roll back slowly

Roll back completely

- Perform 3 sets of 10 crunches. If you have trouble with your balance, place your *tongue on the roof of your mouth*. This stabilizes the neck muscles and will help you work your balance more effectively.

Double Pulley Rotation

The Double Pulley Rotation requires a two-cable rack apparatus as pictured.

- In a semi-squat position, have two pulley cables at chest height. With your *right* arm, grab the pulley *behind* you. With your left hand, grab the pulley in front of you.

Step 1

- Push *forward* with your *right* hand, and pull *back* with your *left*.

Step 2

- Slowly release back to the starting position. Perform 10 repetitions.

- Reverse your grip. With your *left* arm, grab the pulley *behind* you. With your *right* hand, grab the pulley in *front* of you. Perform another 10 repetitions. Perform 3 total sets.

The Tiger Twist

Start the Tiger Twist in a seated position with a soft medicine ball.

- Sit on the ground with your back at a 45-degree incline. Bend your knees to a comfortable position. Your arms need to be straight out in front of you holding a 4 lb. to 10 lb. medicine ball.

Step 1

● *Keeping your arms straight,* rotate the ball as far as you can go.

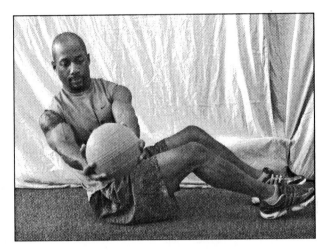

Step 2

● Rotate the ball as far as you can to the other side.

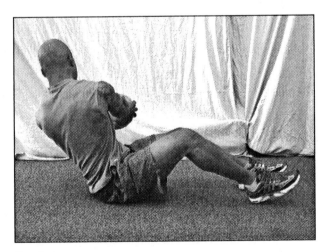

Step 3

● Perform 4 sets of 10 repetitions.

Lat Row

The Lat Row requires an exercise ball and one dumbbell weighing from 4 to 20 lbs.

- Holding a dumbbell in one hand, support your body using the other arm in a straight to slightly bent position on the top of an exercise ball. Your knees should be bent.

Keep your back straight.

Latissimus dorsi muscle

Step 1

- Pull up with your arm. Bring your shoulder blade toward your thoracic spine. Try to feel the latissimus dorsi muscle working.

The exercise ball should be firmly inflated.

Step 2

● Repeat this 10 times with each arm alternating, for a total of 3 sets. Beginners may want to substitute a bench for the ball when getting started and then advance to the exercise ball.

Shoulder Press

The key to performing the Shoulder Press exercise correctly is to focus on balancing on the exercise ball. Start with a lighter weight dumbbell until you can easily balance on the ball.

● Sit on an exercise ball and raise your *left* foot. (You may need to practice your balance first; remember to put your tongue on the roof of your mouth for better balance.) Hold a dumbbell in your right hand next to your right ear.

● Extend your *right* arm while keeping your balance. Start this exercise with 3 to 5 lbs.; if you can't keep your balance, practice with a lighter weight or no weight.

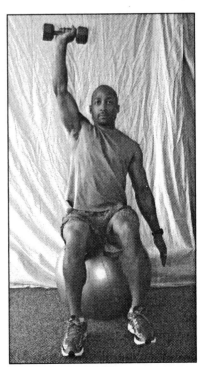

Step 1   Step 2

- Perform 12 repetitions. Then switch to the *left* arm holding the dumbbell and your *right* foot elevated off the floor for a total of 3 sets.

Keep that foot up!

Side view

Balance Squat

The Balance Squat takes the Proper Squat exercise to the next level of challenge for your body. This exercise starts with you standing on a balance board holding a small medicine ball at chest height.

- Using a balance board, try performing a squat. For this exercise, you need to activate your abdominal muscles. Pull your belly button toward your spine.

- Squat down with your weight through your heels. Don't let your knees point together—keep them pointing straight or slightly outward.

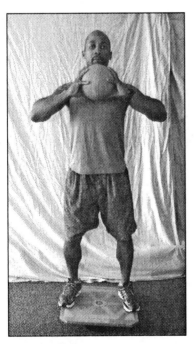
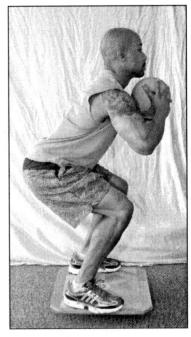

Step 1   Step 2

- Try squatting with or without a 4 to 10lb. medicine ball. Perform 3 sets of 10 to 12 squat repetitions.

Ball Push-ups

Perform a push-up using a large exercise ball. You will notice how much harder these push-ups are because the exercise ball creates an unstable base of support.

- Do a standard push-up with your hands on an unstable base (such as an exercise ball).

For a more challenging exercise, try moving your hands closer together.

Step 1

- *Do not let your back sag.* Perform 3 sets of 10 push-ups.

Step 2

Front view

Seated Rows

For this exercise you'll need a seated row-weight machine or any gym apparatus that has a horizontal cable and a stable support for your feet. It is important to *keep a good curve in your back*. Do not lean forward. Use a handle.

Keep a backward curve in your low back.

Step 1

- Pull back by bringing your shoulder blades together. There should be very little stress on your low back. Your hands should finish at the *middle of your torso height*.

Step 2

- Perform 3 sets of 10 to 12 repetitions.

The Golf Ball

For this exercise you need two dumbbells between 5 lb. and 25 lb. each.

- Take a dumbbell in each hand. Lean forward slightly, and have your feet about shoulder width apart.

Bend at your waist and hips, not with your lumbar spine.

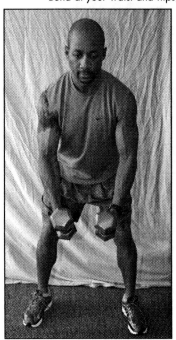
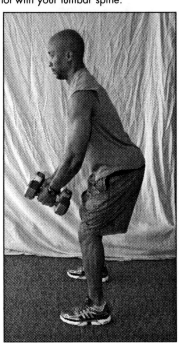

Step 1   Sideview

- Raise the dumbbells above your head as if drawing out a large golf ball in the air.

Step 2

● Slowly bring the dumbbells back to starting position. Perform 3 sets of 10 repetitions.

Hold in front of your head, but not too far.

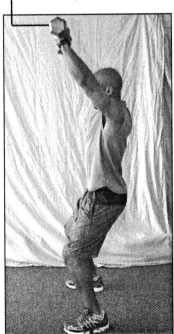

Step 3   Side view

Balance Swing

This exercise requires a large exercise ball and takes some practice, but it will pay off in additional strength.

- Start by practicing your balance while kneeling on the ball. *This may take a few weeks to master.* Simply practice kneeling on the ball five minutes per day. Soon you will be able to balance without much difficulty.

- Once you feel comfortable kneeling on an exercise ball, try a slow golf swing.

Once you feel comfortable, try this exercise with a golf club

The Two-Days-per-Week Schedule

This two-days-per-week schedule is all the *balance* and *strength* training you need to strengthen your core muscles.

This program is designed to take only two days so that you can spend more time on the golf course. However, you can feel free to break up this program into three or four exercise sessions on as many days. And you can always add some of your favorite exercises to this program.

It is always better to perform fewer exercises with correct form than more exercises with poor form. If you feel that your form during an exercise is slipping, stop that exercise—you do not want to develop bad muscle movement patterns.

Begin with fewer total exercises and fewer repetitions. Consider starting at half the number of repetitions and sets, with a plan to build up your strength and coordination. Increase your program repetitions by 10 percent per week.

Endurance is also important to your athletic ability. For a complete exercise program, you need to add three to four days of aerobic exercise each week.

My patients often ask, "What is the best aerobic exercise for me?" I tell them to choose an exercise they enjoy, because then they will do it. Whether it is swimming, cycling, brisk walking, or running, the best exercise is the one you will participate in on a regular basis.

For the best results, participate in aerobic exercise 20 to 40 minutes at least three times per week. The exercise needs to be continuous and should elevate your heart rate. The amount of heart rate elevation will vary per individual.

If you are new to aerobic exercise, you should begin by increasing your heart rate to about 60 percent of your maximum. To calculate this, start 220, subtract your age, and then multiply by 60 percent. At 60 percent of maximum heart rate, you should be able to talk while you are exercising and not get short of breath.

If you have a good aerobic base to work from, bump up your heart rate to 85 percent of its maximum (220 minus your age multiplied by 85 percent).

Building endurance will give you the strength you need to keep proper athletic form on the back nine. Good muscle endurance will also allow your core muscles to support your lumbar spine toward the end of the day. Plus, we all know the benefits of aerobic exercise for our hearts and our general health and well-being.

Program Day #1

Exercise	Equipment	Repetitions	Alternate Limbs	Sets
Squat	4–10 lb. medicine ball 45 lb. bar and up	10–12	No	4
Reverse Lunge	5–10 lb. dumbbells	10	Yes	3
Single Leg Driver Lift	None	8	Yes	3
Hamstring Curls	Exercise ball	8	No/Yes	3
Prone Pitching Wedge	Exercise ball	8	No	3
The Divot Maker	Cables	10	Yes	3
Reverse Divot Maker	Cables	10	Yes	3
Mulligan Twist	Two 20 lb. dumbbells	10	Yes	3
Abdominal Crunch	Exercise ball	10	No	3
Balance Swing	Exercise ball	5 minutes		

Program Day #2

Exercise	Equipment	Repetitions	Alternate Limbs	Sets
Lat Row	Exercise ball 4–20 lb. dumbbell	10	No	3
Seated Row	Row weight machine	10–12	No	3
Ball Push Ups	Exercise ball	8–10	No	3
Tiger Twist	4–10 lb. medicine ball	10	Yes	4
Double Pulley Rotation	Cables	10	Yes	3

Exercise	Equipment	Repetitions	Alternate Limbs	Sets
Shoulder Press	3–15 lb. dumbbells	12	Yes	3
The Golf Ball	5–25 lb. dumbbells	10	No	3
Balance Squat	4–10 lb. medicine ball or dumbbell	10–12	No	3
Abdominal Crunch	Exercise ball	10	No	3
Balance Swing	Medicine ball	5 minutes		

Par for the Course: A Summary

- Functional training emphasizes movement patterns rather than isolating individual muscles.

- Three types of neuromuscular movement are stabilization, locomotor movement, and manipulative motion. All three come into play in the golf swing.

- The most fundamental exercise in functional training is the squat.

- To improve balance while exercising, try resting your tongue on the roof of your mouth.

- Two days a week is enough training for balance and strength.

- The best aerobic exercise is one you like, because you are more likely to do it regularly.

Using Functional Training to Change Your Life: Low Impact

Not everyone is ready to start the program at full speed. Even those who are still golfing may need to begin with a low impact program.

Everyone is different. Age or painful conditions, such as arthritis, may make some of the exercises in the previous chapter seem too challenging. But that does not mean you cannot do something.

The program is also available here in a slightly altered form to accommodate limitations. If any of these exercises cause you to have pain, don't do them! If you merely have a sore muscle for one day after the exercises, you are only getting the rust out of muscles that need to be strengthened.

Balance Training

As we age we slowly lose our sense of balance. Balance training exercises can help you regain what you may have lost. Balance training takes just five minutes each day. Practice on a burst-resistant exercise ball for best results.

- Sit on a ball that is well filled with air. Sit up straight, keeping a normal curve in your low back.
- Your head should be held tall and your abdominal muscles tight.

Step 1   Step 2

- Hold out your arms with your palms facing forward. Lift up one leg, and maintain that same sitting posture. Try this for 30 seconds, and then switch legs.

Step 3

- Try sitting on the ball with both legs out in front of you. Balance takes time to learn, so give yourself a week to learn how to sit on the ball. Try to practice your balance training for 5 minutes each day.

- Remember that balance training takes only 5 minutes each day.

Step 4

The Adaptive Squat

The adaptive squat is designed for individuals whose knees do not have a full and comfortable range of motion due to "wear and tear" changes or arthritis. This squat is the same as the Proper Squat described in Chapter 9, except that you do not need to bend your knees as much.

Hold your exercise ball in front of you. Your feet should be shoulder-width apart with your toes facing forward.

- Fold at your hips into a seated position. Hold your abdominal muscles tight. Your weight needs to be going through your heels. Squat down as far as comfortable (approximately 70 degrees at the knees, as pictured).

Step 1

Step 2

- Push up through your heels, feeling your muscles contract in your abdominal muscles and your buttock muscles. Perform 2 to 3 sets of 10 squatting exercises.

Abdominal Crunches

These crunches are the same as the Abdominal Crunches in Chapter 9, except for a few changes in positioning.

- Center the ball on your lower or middle thoracic region. You can cross your arms over your chest.

Step 1

- Pull your navel toward your spine, and roll your torso upward starting from your head to your neck to your torso. Don't bend way over the ball. Finish when you can no longer roll any further without lifting yourself off the ball.

Step 2

- Reverse the rolling to finish the exercise. Try holding your hands at your ears to make this exercise more challenging. Perform 3 sets of 10 crunches.

Step 3

- Abdominal exercises can be performed every day.

The Bridge

This is a wonderful stabilization exercise for your back.

- Lie on your back with your arms out to your sides. Have your palms facing up. Bend your knees so that your feet are flat on the ground.

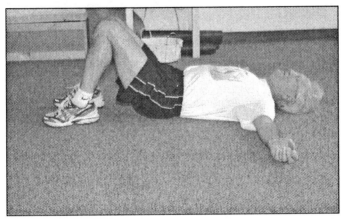

Step 1

- Raise your butt up off the ground until your back is straight, and hold for two seconds.

Step 2

- Slowly let your butt back down to touch the ground, and then repeat the exercise. Perform 3 sets of 10 Bridges. When you get the hang of this exercise, try it using the exercise ball.

Step 3

- Rest the ball on the lower portion of your calf muscles, repeat the bridge exercise. Perform 2 sets of 10 Bridge exercises.

Step 4

- Don't be too shy to ask for a little help with your balance.

The Twist

Motion is lotion! This is a great warm-up exercise. The rotational motion warms up the joints of your back as well as all the rotational joints used in the golf swing. Warm joints are well lubricated: The warm joint fluid flows better to protect your joints.

- Stand with the ball held out straight in front of you. Have your legs spread about shoulder-width apart. Be sure to have a little bend in your knees.

- Rotate as far as *comfortable* to the right, keeping your arms as straight as possible. It is all right to pivot your left leg a little.

Step 1

Step 2

- Rotate as far as comfortable to the left, allowing for a little right-knee rotation if needed. Start with 2 sets of 10. Try to advance to one full rotation for every year of your age.

- For an added stretch, lift the ball over your head and back down with no torso rotation. Perform this for 2 sets of 20. Be sure to keep a little bend in your knees.

Step 3

Step 4

Stork Test

The Stork Test is designed for you to test your progress with your balance.

- Stand with your arms crossed across your chest. Lift your right leg up, and balance on your left leg. Then perform the Stork using your other leg. The goal is to be able to keep your balance for 30 seconds.

- For a real challenge, try this with your eyes closed for 30 seconds. The stork not only tests your balance but also helps you develop awareness of your body and its surroundings (proprioception).

Step 1

Step 2

Par for the Course: A Summary

- Start exercises with balance training.
- Balance training takes only 5 minutes per day.
- If an exercise causes pain, back off.
- When you squat, bring your legs to a 70-degree angle bend at the knees instead of 90 degrees.
- During abdominal crunches, do not bend backward over the ball.

Stretching on the First Tee

The body is designed to stretch only so far. There is an anatomic end point, which is as far as your body can move in any direction because of bony blocks.

The body also has a physiological endpoint, which is how far you are comfortable going. For a good athlete, the difference between the anatomic endpoint and the physiological endpoint is minimal.

People with poor flexibility have a short physiological endpoint. Golfers with poor flexibility still want to attack the ball, so they push past the physiological endpoint repetitively—and that can become painful.

Stretching out that physiological endpoint before your first swing is a much better idea. *Warming up* literally means warming up the body tissues. The heat comes from an increased heart rate, which sends more blood to the muscles. This increases the metabolic rate and, yes, the temperature of the tissues.

The increased blood flow and warmth make muscles more flexible and resilient to injury. Stretching helps your movements become smoother and more coordinated.

On the other hand, athletically activating muscles without first stretching them, as in swinging a driver on the first tee, could cause injury. That is why stretching is so important.

Stretching Is Part of Conditioning

Stretching means going through a certain range of motions so that your joints, muscles, tendons, and ligaments are used to the movement. That way, when you do it again more suddenly, your body will be ready. If you stretch through certain ranges of motion on a regular basis, your body gets used to that stretching and that stress.

Stretching gives you a better range of motion and makes it easier for you to move and to use proper body mechanics. For instance, if your knees are stiff and you can't squat down, it will be difficult to squat and (see Chapter 7) pick up an object properly.

There are certain stretches for the back that we just don't do naturally during a day—such as bending backward. It is important to challenge your body, especially if you are a golfer, because the phrase "Use it or lose it" contains a certain amount of wisdom.

Use it or lose it?

Well, even if you haven't used it, you haven't lost it as long as you begin using it.

The Healing Power of Stretching: A Story

For six weeks before she came to me, the pain had been bothering Mrs. B. She is a nice lady in her 60s.

She came to my office with complaints of severe leg pain, from her low back all the way to her foot. It went through her buttocks, her thigh, and down her calf. Prior to this leg pain developing, she had LBP off and on for years, but she had managed it well enough that she always participated in many activities, including golf.

During her first visit with me, after some tests, I watched her movements and then designed one specific stretch. In addition, I gave her a list of dos and don'ts having to do with posture and body mechanics. But the key was the stretch.

After a couple of weeks, she came back and said that the problem had lessened but the pain was still severe. It forced her to modify her activities.

During another office visit, I tried a lumbar rotation manipulation that gave her a better range of motion and allowed her to do one movement she was unable to do earlier. I sent her to physical therapy to learn stretching that mimicked the lumbar rotation I did in the clinic. She also received spinal manipulation treatments in physical therapy. Now Mrs. B. had two stretches to work with at home.

A week later, the pain in her leg had lessened.

In a few more visits to physical therapy, she learned a couple more stretches, and her leg pain disappeared. She still has some LBP, but that is also under control thanks to a stretching and strengthening regimen.

Of course, Mrs. B. was diligent and stuck with the program even when results were slow in coming. Healing is a process. And now Mrs. B., inspired by the results of stretching, plans to work on core stabilization exercises as she begins to learn functional training.

Once you learn the power of your body, you can't help but believe. Of course, it's still up to you.

Listen to Your Body

Stretching will most likely cause you some discomfort. That does not mean you should stop. You have to be able to differentiate between different kinds of pain, because stretch soreness is good. It means you have begun to challenge muscles and make them work for you.

But if you feel a specific pain come on while you are doing an activity, you should back off. How do you know the difference? You have to listen to your body:

- A stretch should not cause any sharp pain.
- It shouldn't cause any lingering pain.
- It shouldn't cause any pain that shoots down your leg.

Delayed muscle soreness is to be expected, even up to a day or two after you exercise. It is normal when you start out to feel a bit of soreness from the new challenges.

If you do a stretch or an exercise and you have no pain during or immediately afterward but then develop pain a day or so later, please consider what other activities you have done in between. Don't be quick to blame exercise. Exercise and stretching are good.

Start Stretching at the First Tee

For the warm-up to be most effective, start stretching at the first tee. This simple stretching program can be performed in 5 to 10 minutes. Waiting 15 to 20 minutes between stretching and the first tee allows your muscles to get cold. This stretching program begins from top to bottom, so grab a club and let's go.

Warming up is a transition phase between being sedentary and being active. Thus you need to start slowly. And you must avoid forceful bouncing.

Each stretch *should be held* for 30 to 45 seconds. *Do not bounce. Bouncing while stretching can cause injuries.*

Fingers and Wrist Stretch

- While standing, interlock your fingers and face your palms up.
- Reach to the sky, feeling the stretch through your arms, shoulders, back, and legs. For a little extra effort, stand on your tip-toes.

Fingers and wrist stretch

Shoulder Pull Behind the Head

- While holding the head of a golf club (say, a sand wedge), hold one of your arms up behind your head.

- With your other arm, reach behind your back and grab the handle of the club. Pull gently on the handle in a downward direction. You should feel the stretch in the arm that is holding the club head. Hold this stretch for 30 seconds, and then switch arms.

Shoulder pull behind the head stretch   Back view

Straight Arm Across the Chest

- With one arm straight, bring it across your chest just below collarbone height.

- Fold your opposite arm around your straightened arm, just in front of your elbow.

- Pull the straightened elbow towards your folded arm's shoulder, and hold for 30 seconds. Switch arms, and hold the stretch for 30 seconds.

Arm across the chest stretch

Torso and Back Rotation

- Hold a club behind your head and across your shoulders. Your legs should be positioned as if addressing a golf ball on a tee.

- Rotate your shoulders into a backswing, and hold for two seconds.

● Rotate your shoulders as if swinging your club, and come to rest at your golf swing follow-through position. Hold for two seconds. Be sure to rotate your hips and rear foot. Your spine should remain straight the entire time as you rotate around your spine.

Step 1

Step 2

Step 3

Inner Thigh Stretch:

● Holding a club with both hands, spread your feet wide apart and bend forward as if trying to touch your toes.

● Bend one knee, and lean to the side towards that knee. You will feel a stretch in the inner thigh of the straight leg.

● With your arms straight, rotate your shoulders toward the bent knee side until the club is perpendicular to the ground. Hold this stretch for 30 seconds.

● Rotate back to the toe-touch position, and perform this stretch bending the opposite leg.

Step 1

Step 2

Step 3

Quadriceps Stretch

Support yourself with a club for balance. Bend the *opposite* leg and try to touch your butt with your heel. You should feel the stretch through the front of your thigh. Be sure to hold your chest up and look forward toward the horizon. Hold this stretch for 30 seconds, and then switch legs.

Quadriceps stretch

Back of Leg Stretch

- Step one foot forward and the opposite foot back. For balance, hold a golf club in the hand of the back foot.

- Lean your pelvis forward with *your chest up,* and keep your back foot *heel on the ground.* You will feel the stretch in your back leg calf. Hold this stretch for 30 to 45 seconds.

- Lean forward, and try to touch your front foot toes with your free (on the same side) hand. Hold this stretch for 30 to 45 seconds. Switch leg positions and switch the hand holding the club, and repeat the stretching exercise.

Step 1

Step 2

Stretching While on the Course

There is a good stretch to perform *during* your golf game. In the golf swing of right-handed golfers, more force is generated in the counterclockwise direction. This counterclockwise rotation can create a muscular torsion or rotation pattern to the left. To balance out this muscle torsion or muscle memory, it is good to stretch your musculature in the clockwise direction.

Every third or fourth hole, take a few practice swings in the opposite direction. This will help unwind any torsion patterns that build up in your lumbar spine.

Par for the Course: A Summary

- Warming up literally means warming up the body tissues, which makes them more flexible and resilient to injury.

- Stretching simply means going through a certain range of motions so that your joints, muscles, tendons, and ligaments are used to the motion.

- A stretch should not cause any sharp pain, lingering pain, or pain shooting down your leg.

- Stretching gives you a better range of motion and should make it easier to use proper body mechanics.

- Stretching should be done shortly before you begin exercising.

- Never bounce. Hold your stretch for 30 to 45 seconds.

Conclusion:
Motion Is Life

I noticed early in my life that exercise always made me feel good. When I was stressed out or sad, a good session always made me feel better. Exercise was always dependable, and it never let me down.

And that is how I came upon my credo: Motion is life.

Yet we all know that health can be fleeting. As every breath is precious, so is every motion. I believe that movement is part of what we are as humans—whether the motion is subtle or extreme. All motion is intense because life is intense. And the better our bodies are able to function, the more we can enjoy all aspects of life.

Stay Forever Young

You can feel younger. If you live now, you know that health is relative in a way that says *50 can feel like 40.*

And therefore, 60 can feel like 50, and 70 can feel like 60, and so on. Living longer is no longer the key to a happy life. We all want to live *better.* We want a better quality of life. Hobbling through our 70s and 80s hurting and not feeling well is not the quality of life we are looking for. We want to feel golden during our golden years.

The aging phenomenon does not start in our 50s and 60s. In my practice, I see the aging process begin to take its toll on individuals starting at age 35. People who do not exercise start to have chronic musculoskeletal pain in their late 30s.

Anti-aging medicine practitioners are using hormonal supplements, a lot of vitamins, and dietary changes to make their patients feel better. But the most effective way to stay young and feel good is to participate in a daily exercise program that incorporates strength training and aerobic training.

In my practice, my 60-year-old patients and my 80-year-old patients are interchangeable. I have 80-year-old patients who look great, feel great, and are asking me for Viagra. And I have many 60-year-old patients who are ready to go out to pasture.

What is the difference between these two patient populations? My young 80-year-old patients exercise.

Motion is life.

A Golfer's Story

Like many patients, Frank entered my office looking for a quick fix for his back pain—a magic pill, a special injection, and voila, the pain would disappear. Frank soon learned, however, that it was he, not I, who would do the healing.

At 72, two fears haunted Frank. He feared giving up golf, but more than that, he feared playing golf. Every time he played, he hurt, which made him suspect that golf was the cause of his pain.

He thought that if he hurt while playing golf, his back probably suffered with every golf swing. By the time he came to see me, his pain ranged from a dull ache to a sharp pain across his low back and into his right buttock. He occasionally felt pain in his right hamstring region.

An x-ray showed that Frank had developed significant arthritis in his lower lumbar spine joints. When I asked him to squat, he displayed poor form; and when I asked him to balance on one foot, he struggled to maintain balance for more than a few seconds. I saw room for improvement.

But the only magic pill I could offer was the combination of work and time. Only hard work would reverse the muscle dysfunction and poor posture that Frank developed over the years. First, I sent Frank for a few sessions of physical therapy to get his mind in touch with his back, pelvic, and abdominal muscles. Once he learned what to activate and how, I sent Frank to a personal trainer to learn about functional training.

Eight weeks after his first visit, Frank returned to my office smiling. His back felt better. He had benefited greatly from the physical therapy and from three sessions per week of functional training. There was new ease to his golf swing, and he was hitting the ball 15 yards farther on his drives, he said.

Frank's story proves again: Motion is life.

Play Golf Forever

You are older now, and a bit wiser. You understand your body better than anyone, but reeducating yourself on the power of exercise is at the core of this program.

Exercise really can be a magic bullet. It takes more than one session, and the cure doesn't happen all at once. However, a program of these best exercises on Earth, if you stick to it, can make a difference in many aspects of your life, including your golf game.

Do you have low back pain? As I've explained, there are many possible causes and treatments. But at the core of most causes and cures is the patient's commitment, or lack of commitment, to exercise as well as to proper body mechanics.

This program pays attention to the core muscles of your abdomen and back, and you build a power cylinder around your spine. Then you can begin to take stress off the structure of your spine.

This works. The body has an innate power to heal itself. In a relatively short time, you will start to notice a lessening of back pain and an improvement in the way you move and function on a daily basis.

No matter your condition, you can become more athletic. It's true; athleticism can still be achieved no matter what your age. Athleticism is achieved by programming your body to move correctly. Correct movements are learned as movement patterns. Your neuromuscular system is trainable and adaptable. If you program proper movement patterns into your neuromuscular system through exercise, your body will respond with athletic movements.

The cliché is true: Practice makes perfect.

Core strengthening through functional training is an exercise program that emphasizes these athletic movements. These exercises are performed utilizing balance and rotational movement patterns. In doing them, you train your neuromuscular system to work, and move, better.

With this program, you will improve the way your neuromuscular system functions. This improved function applies to your golf game, to all sports, and of course to everyday life. With correctly developed movement patterns, you will be able to recreate that perfect stroke to improve your golf game. A proper stroke will also prevent injuries.

Just listen to your body during exercise. If you are sore for a day or two after exercising, then you are challenging your muscles, and your soreness will become less and less over time. If you hurt during exercise, or you are going to the point when you cannot perform an exercise, you are pushing too much. If you hurt three to four days after exercise, then you have also pushed it too much.

If all of these exercises cause you significant pain, you should see a physician or physical therapist to assist you in physical therapy and pain management.

Stretching is also an important part of exercise. All golfers should stretch before the first tee. Stretching increases blood flow and lengthens the muscles, allowing for better function. Warm muscles are less brittle and have a lesser tendency to strain and tear with activity. Given the acceleration and twisting forces in the golf stroke, stretching is a must.

An added bonus of stretching is the lengthening of tight, cold muscles. Elongated and warm muscles will help you generate the maximum amount of force in your golf swing due to a better lever arm, or fulcrum, of motion. Warmed-up muscles also respond better to signals your brain is sending to your muscular system, giving you athleticism.

With athleticism of movement comes improved efficiency of motion. This translates into less muscle fatigue and increased physical endurance.

You will also gain strength with functional training. When strength, muscle coordination, and endurance are increased, there is much less risk to your joints and spine.

It's pretty simple, really. If your back hurts, don't complain—do something about it. Motion is life. Get some exercise.

I used to tell them, but now it's my patients who report back to me: "You can play golf forever!"

Par for the Course: A Summary

- Motion is life.
- The body has an innate ability to heal itself.
- The most effective way to stay young and feel good is to participate in a daily exercise program that incorporates strength training and aerobic training.
- The exercise program taught in this book pays attention to the core muscles of your abdomen and back, giving you the tools to build a power cylinder around your spine.

- If you program proper movement patterns into your neuromuscular system through exercise, your body will respond with athletic movements.

- Stretching increases blood flow and lengthens the muscles, allowing for better function.

- If your back hurts, you can do something about it.

- You can play golf forever.

Bibliography

Alfieri, Rosemarie Gioonta. *Functional Training: Everyone's Guide to the New Fitness Revolution.* New York: Hatherleigh Press, 2001.

Boden, Scott. "Abnormal Magnetic-Resonance Scans of the Lumbar Spine in Asymptomatic Patients." *The Journal of Bone and Joint Surgery* 3 (March 1990): 403-408.

Deyo, Richard. "Low Back Pain." *The New England Journal of Medicine* 344, no. 5 (February 2001): 363-370.

Evans, C. "A study to investigate whether golfers with a history of low back pain show a reduced endurance of the transverse abdominis." *Journal of Manual and Manipulative Therapy* 8 (2000): 162-174.

Frymoyer, J. "Back Pain and Sciatica." *The New England Journal of Medicine* 318, no. 5 (February 1988): 292-298.

Grimshaw, Paul. "Case Report: Reduction of Low Back Pain in a Professional Golfer." Medicine & Science in Sports and Exercise 32, no. 10 (2000): 1667-1673.

Hetu, Fred. "Effects of Conditioning on Physical Fitness and Club Head Speed in Mature Golfers." *Perceptual and Motor Skills* 86 (1998): 811-815.

Horton, John. "Abdominal muscle activation of elite male golfers with chronic low back pain." *Medicine & Science in Sports and Exercise* 33, no. 10 (2001): 1647-1654.

Hosea, Timothy. "Back Pain in Golf." *Clinics in Sports Medicine* 15, no. 1 (January 1996): 37-52.

Johnsson, Karl. "The Natural Course of Lumbar Spinal Stenosis." *Clinical Orthopedics and Related research* 279 (June 1992): 82-86.

Kalb, Claudia. "The Great Back Debate." *Newsweek* (April 26, 2004).

Koslow, Robert. "Patterns of Weight Shift in the Swings of Beginning Golfers." *Perceptual and Motor Skills* 79 (October1994): 1296-1298.

Kottke, Frederic. "From Reflex to Skill: The Training of Coordination." *Archives of Physical Medicine and Rehabilitation* 61 (December 1980): 551-561.

Libkuman, Terry. "Training in Timing Improves Accuracy in Golf." *The Journal of General Psychology* 129, no. 1 (2002): 77-96.

Lindsay, D. "Comparison of spine motion in elite golfers with and without low back pain." *Journal of Sports Sciences* 20 (2002): 599-605.

McCarroll, John. "Overuse Injuries of the Upper Extremity in Golf." *Clinics in Sports Medicine* 20, no. 3 (July 2001): 146-149.

O'Sullivan, Susan. *Physical Rehabilitation Laboratory Manual: Focus on Functional Training.* Philadelphia: F.A. Davis Co., 1999.

Parkkari, J. "A controlled trial of the health benefits of regular walking on a golf course." *American Journal of Medicine* 109, no. 2 (2000): 102-10.

Pink, Marilyn. "Preventive Exercises in Golf." *Clinics in Sports Medicine* 15, no. 1 (1996):147-162.

Saal, Jeffrey and Joel S. Saal. "Intradiscal Electrothermal Treatment for Chronic Discogenic Low Back Pain." *Spine* 27, no. 8 (2002): 966-974.

Steven, J. "Surgical and Nonsurgical Management of Sciatica Secondary to a Lumbar Disc Herniation: Five-year Outcomes From the Maine Lumbar Spine Study." *Spine* 26 (2001): 1179-1187.

Steven, J. "The Maine Lumbar Spine Study Part III: 1-year Outcomes of Surgical and Nonsurgical Management of Lumbar Spinal Stenosis." *Spine* 21 (1996): 1787-1794.

Theriault, Germain. "Golf Injuries: an Overview." *Journal of Sports Medicine* 1 (July 26, 1998): 43-57.

Glossary

addressing the ball

Facing the golf ball and getting set up for the golf swing.

athleticism

Movement patterns that contain strength, agility, flexibility, and endurance. These movement patterns can be applied to everyday living as well as sports.

atrophy

Wasting away of muscle tissue due to disease or disuse.

core strengthening

Strengthening of the torso and pelvic musculature. Strong core muscles allow movement to be transferred to your arms and legs by first stabilizing your body's center of gravity. Core strengthening generates force of movement by coordinating motion of your limbs and torso.

corticospinal tracts

Specialized nerve tracts in the spinal cord that carry movement messages from the brain to the nerves that exit the spine.

cyst

An anatomically common sac- or bladder-like structure that contains fluid.

disc annulus

The outer two-thirds of a spinal disc made up of a tough connective tissue. Tears in this tissue can be painful.

engram

A pattern of movement that has been memorized by the muscles, nerves, and brain of an individual. These movement patterns (such as a golf swing) may be repeated without cognitive thought once an engram has been formed.

ESI

Epidural steroid injection (ESI). A steroid injection placed in the space just outside the spinal canal so that the nerve roots can be reached. Epidural steroids are used to treat inflammation of the nerve roots caused by herniated discs.

facet

A joint of the spine. Facets have a joint lining and joint fluid and can become inflamed just like a larger joint such as a knee joint.

flexibility

Ability of body tissues to bend and stretch easily.

functional training

Exercises that integrate balance and muscular stability during the exertion of muscular force. These exercises often mimic specific activities that the practitioner wants to improve.

HNP

Herniated Nucleus Pulposis. Condition where the outer two-thirds of the disc annulus tears and the inner one-third of the disc (nucleus pulposis) leaks out of the disc. This nucleus pulposis is an irritant to nerve tissue and is the main cause of nerve root irritations. HNPs can be an incidental finding. It may be found in 20 to 30 percent of people age 30 to 60 who have no back pain.

IDET

Intradiscal Electrothermal Treatment. An interventional radiologic procedure where a heated wire is inserted into a painful disc, thereby destroying the small nerves that give that disc sensation. Also called Intradiscal Electrothermal Therapy.

lumbar spine

The five vertebrae that form your low back. The lumbar region is the part of your spine that is below your ribs and above your pelvis.

MRI

Magnetic Resonance Image. A diagnostic study during which a large magnet takes a picture of anatomic structures. It is used to visualize bone, muscles, tendons, cartilage, brain, nerves, and essentially all soft tissue with good clarity.

muscles

- **deltoid**—Triangular muscle located on the lateral portion of your shoulder.

- **external abdominal obliques**—Abdominal muscles that make up the side walls of your abdomen. These fibers run diagonally downward from your side to your belly button.

- **gluteus maximus**—Your butt muscles. These are the most powerful muscles of the body.

- **hamstrings**—Muscles located on the back of your thigh. These muscles bend your knee but straighten your hips.

- **internal abdominal obliques**—Abdominal muscles that make up the inner layer of your abdominal wall. These muscle fibers run in the opposite direction of the external abdominal obliques.

- **latissimus dorsi**—The broadest muscles of the body. They give body builders that nice V-shape to their backs. The mid- to low-back muscle pulls your arms and shoulder blades downward.

- **paraspinals**—Muscles that surround your lumbar spine. These muscles run up and down your spine in a vertical manner and support the spine. These are usually the muscles involved in low back pain from muscle spasms.

- **pectoralis**—Chest muscles that attach from the center of your chest to your upper arm.

- **pyriformis**—Muscle shaped like a triangle that runs from the sacrum to the side of your hips, running under your larger buttock muscles. The sciatic nerve runs under the pyriformis muscle and can be pinched by a muscle spasm.

- **quadraceps**—Muscles located on the front of your thigh. These muscles straighten your knee and your hips.

- **rectus abdominus**—Muscles that form the center of your abdomen. These are your "six-pack" muscles,

- **transversus abdominus**—Sheet of muscle that runs across your lower abdomen. This is the cornerstone muscle for core strengthening.

muscle dysfunction

A state of painful muscles due to muscular imbalance, overused muscles from poor posture, underused muscles that have become tight and weak, or injured muscles that are in chronic spasm. Chronic pain from muscle dysfunction is a common problem.

muscle spindle fiber

Specialized muscle fibers within the body of the muscle that send sensory information to the spinal cord. These fibers act as control centers of the muscle.

myofascial pain / Myofascial Pain Syndrome (MPS)

A painful musculoskeletal condition, and a common cause of musculoskeletal pain. MPS is characterized by the development of tender pea-size areas of the muscles called myofascial trigger points. These trigger points are locally tender when active and refer pain through specific patterns to other areas of the body. A trigger point can develop due to any number of causes such as trauma, overuse, and poor posture. Trigger points are usually associated with a taut band—a ropy thickening of the muscle tissue. Typically, a trigger point, when pressed, causes pain to be felt elsewhere. This is called *referred pain.*

NSAIDs

Non-Steroidal Anti-Inflammatory Drugs. Medications that, in addition to having pain-relieving (analgesic) effects, reduce inflammation. Motrin, Aleve, and Ibuprofen are available as over-the-counter drugs or by prescription. Many other NSAIDs are available by presription. The NSAIDs work by affecting chemicals in the body that cause inflammation, the *prostaglandins.*

Nucleoplasty

Similar to IDET, but uses radio frequencies to destroy the painful nerves inside the disc.

nucleus pulposis

The inner third of a disc, formed of a gelatinous material. This material is irritating to spinal nerves and leads to an inflammatory response. This is the material that leaks out of a herniated disc.

osteoarthritis

Wear and tear of the cartilage and bones of joints. This process may be due to age, previous trauma, rheumatic diseases, or a genetic predisposition to arthritis. Arthritic joints may be actively inflamed and painful or not painful at all.

physical therapy

Services provided by physical therapists that help restore function, improve mobility, relieve pain, and prevent or limit permanent physical disabilities of patients suffering from injuries or disease. It restores, maintains, and promotes overall fitness and health. Physical therapy patients include accident victims and individuals with disabling conditions such as low back pain, arthritis, heart disease, fractures, head injuries, and cerebral palsy.

physical training

The use of exercise to improve physical function and athletic perfor-mance. Physical training is associated with increases in muscle strength, power, endurance, and flexibility of the musculoskeletal sys-tem and better performance of the nervous system.

Pilates

An exercise system focused on improving flexibility and strength for the total body. The Pilates Method was developed in the 1920s by the physical trainer and founder of the Pilates Studio method, Joseph H. Pilates. Pilates is a series of controlled movements engaging the body and mind, performed on specifically designed exercise apparatus and taught by certified practitioners.

pronation

Rotation of the hands and forearms so the palms are downward.

proprioception

The perception of your body parts in time, space, and angular veloc-ity by your brain. Essentially, it is your awareness of your body in terms of posture, movement, equilibrium, and position. These sensa-tions are perceived through the small nerve receptors in your joints, tendons, and muscles.

prostaglandin

One of a number of hormone-like substances that participate in a wide range of body functions such as the contraction and relaxation of smooth muscle, the dilation and constriction of blood vessels, con-trol of blood pressure, and modulation of inflammation.

radiculopathy

Inflammation of the nerve roots as they branch off the spinal cord. This may be caused by herniated discs, arthritis of the spine, diabetes mellitus, or trauma; sometimes no cause is found.

radiofrequency ablation

An interventional radiologic procedure during which the nerves that supply the joints of the spine are destroyed using high-frequency radio waves. A radiofrequency lesion is created by passing current through an electrode to raise the tissue temperature to 60 to 80 degrees centigrade for 60 to 90 seconds. Regeneration of these nerves occurs over time.

rotator cuff

Deep muscles that surround the shoulder joints and hold them together. These muscles rotate the shoulder inward and outward.

sciatic nerve

The combination of the fifth lumbar and first sacral nerve that form the largest nerve in the body. This nerve runs through the middle of the buttock cheek and down the posterior thigh and calf muscles and ends in the foot and toes. There is one on each side of the body.

sciatica

Irritation or inflammation of the sciatic nerve due to any cause.

somatic dysfunction

Impaired or altered function of related components of the somatic (body framework) system; skeletal, arthrodial, and myofascial structures; and related vascular, lymphatic, and neural elements. In general terms, somatic dysfunction can be thought of as a poor alignment of bony structures and muscular imbalances.

spinal stenosis

Narrowing of the spinal canal due to arthritis of the spine, disc bulges, or thickening of the spinal ligaments. Spinal stenosis often causes bilateral leg pain with standing and walking that is relieved by sitting down.

transforaminal injection

Like an epidural steroid injection, but done with x-ray guidance. The nerve root is accessed through the bony exit of the spine called the *neuroforamen*.

Index

Printed in the United States
56552LVS00001B/6

9 781933 669007